Contents

■ ■ ■

Content Guidance

■ ■ ■

Questions and Answers

Introduction

About this guide

This guide has been written for students preparing for Module 2591 of the OCR A2 History specification. The module is entitled 'Themes in History 1793–1996', and the option covered in this guide is 'Russian Dictatorship 1855–1956'. This period of Russian history begins with the accession to the imperial throne of Tsar Alexander II during the Crimean War in 1855, and ends with the emergence of Nikita Khrushchev as the effective leader of the Soviet Union by 1956, after a period of jostling for power among Soviet leaders following the death of Stalin in 1953.

This is a guide rather than a textbook. Its aim is to provide an outline of the major themes running through modern Russian history during this 100-year period. The aim is *not* to provide a detailed chronology or narrative; space does not permit that. In any case, a detailed 'blow-by-blow' account of Russian history during this period is not required. To quote from the OCR specification:

> The question papers are very different in concept because they take a perspective, broad-brush, overview of the century-long period. Their objective is the perception of patterns, with the focus on the causes and consequences of continuity, development and change over the full period of the Key Theme.

The focus is on the *longer-term perspective* and the key words are *causation*, *development*, *change* and *continuity*.

This guide is intended primarily as a *revision* tool. It is recommended that you work through the book theme by theme. After studying and revising each major theme in the Content Guidance section, you should attempt the relevant essay question in the Question and Answer section. The best practice (although one which requires a certain amount of self-discipline) is to write the essay under exam conditions, i.e. in 45 minutes, and then to assess it, awarding marks or grades by consulting the relevant mark schemes and worked responses.

The specification

The specification gives in broad outline the type of approach required and the main content to be covered:

> This theme focuses on the nature of Russian government and its impact on the Russian people and society. Candidates should understand the similarities and differences between the autocratic rule of the tsars to 1917 and the communist dictatorship established in that year. Candidates are expected to have an understanding of the causes and consequences of the February and October revolutions, but **not** a detailed knowledge of the events of 1917.

Content

- The development of tsarist autocracy to 1917, the impact of reforms and reactionary policies, the causes of the 1917 revolutions.
- The growth of opposition: its extent and effectiveness both before and after 1917.
- The development of a communist dictatorship from 1917: the reasons for the development of a totalitarian regime.
- The impact of the dictatorial nature of government on the economy and society of the Russian empire and the USSR.

Candidates are **not** expected to demonstrate a detailed understanding of the specification content but are expected to have a knowledge of the main developments and turning points relevant to the theme.

The format and requirements of the OCR examination

The exam is 1 hour and 30 minutes long and counts for 20% of the overall A-level grade. Three essay questions are set, with a maximum of 60 marks for each. Each question tests knowledge of a different theme. You must answer *any two* essay questions. The phrasing of the questions will require you to demonstrate a knowledge and understanding of the 100-year period rather than focus on a specific event. For example, you will not be asked to explain the motives behind Stalin's purges in the 1930s. Rather, you might be asked to assess the extent to which the purges fit into the pattern of the treatment of potential threats to various regimes, tsarist-autocratic and Soviet, during the 100-year period.

To assist you during the exam, OCR will supply a chronology outlining the major dates and events in Russian history between 1855 and 1956 with your exam paper.

You should show a breadth of historical understanding in your essays. You are reminded of this in the rubric on the exam paper: 'Answers are required to demonstrate understanding of the processes of historical continuity, development and change across the full breadth of the period studied.'

The guidance given by OCR on what is meant by 'full breadth' is as follows:

Assertions, analysis and evaluation must be substantiated with examples of relevant fact, but examiners are looking primarily for history in breadth — for evidence of an understanding of the 'big picture'.

- In what ways were the elements of the theme different at the end of the period from the ways each had been at the start of the period and why?
- To what extent had things remained the same across the period and why?
- Was the pace of change roughly constant or distinctly uneven and why?
- What were the consequences of those individual continuities and changes, and of the overall balance between them when immutability or innovation, reaction or reform, predominated?

Only when candidates understand the patterns will they be able to construct in each essay an effective developmental account.

The nature of the option and module, and the wording of some of the questions, can invite a broadly chronological approach in essays. This can work well, but the danger is that essays can become too 'narrative' and descriptive. If a broadly chronological approach is adopted, care must be taken to ensure that the essay remains focused and analytical. The focus should at all times be on pointing out the key similarities/differences/causes and consequences of the subject matter of the essay.

The mark schemes

When marking scripts, examiners have two mark schemes: a 'generic' and a 'subject specific' mark scheme. Of the two, the generic mark scheme is by far the more important.

The examiner's first task after marking an essay is to put it into one of the bands. The mark scheme gives an indication of the typical features to be expected in each band. It is important to realise that this is intended for guidance only. Clearly, in a subject like history there can be no definitive, rigid or prescriptive requirements for each grade. Therefore, it is unlikely that an essay will fulfil all the requirements of any particular band exactly. There might, for example, be aspects of both bands I and II in an essay. It is the 'best fit' which is important. Once the examiner has decided on which band to fit the essay into, he or she will then go immediately to the middle of the band. Most of the bands have a range of 5 marks, although band I has 12 marks. The 'fine tuning' of marks within each band is done according to the quality of argument and analysis, range of examples and use of English.

The generic mark scheme is a crucial document since it sets out clearly what the examiners are looking for. It is very detailed and you should be fully aware of the requirements for each band. Learning the contents of the mark scheme is as important as revising the content of the module in preparation for the exam.

The generic mark scheme
Band I: 48–60 marks
The response is not perfect but the best that a candidate can be expected to achieve at A2 in examination conditions. There may be some unevenness, but the demands of the question (e.g. causation, change over time, evaluation) are fully addressed. The answer demonstrates a high level of ability to synthesise elements to reflect the synoptic nature of the unit. The approach is consistently analytical or explanatory rather than descriptive or narrative. The answer is fully relevant. The argument is structured coherently and supported by very appropriate factual material. Ideas are expressed fluently and clearly. At the lower end of the band, there may be some weaker sections but the overall quality nonetheless shows the candidate is in control of the argument. The writing is fluent and uses appropriate historical vocabulary. The answer shows accuracy in grammar, punctuation and spelling.

Band II: 42–47 marks

The answer demonstrates clearly the ability to synthesise elements to reflect the synoptic nature of the unit. There is a good awareness of change and/or continuity and/or development over the necessary extended period. The response is focused clearly on the demands of the question, but there is some unevenness. The approach is mostly analytical or explanatory rather than descriptive or narrative. Most of the argument is structured coherently and supported by very appropriate factual material. The answer is fully relevant. The impression is that a good solid answer has been provided. Most of the writing is fluent and uses appropriate historical vocabulary. The answer mostly shows accuracy in grammar, punctuation and spelling.

Band III: 36–41 marks

The answer demonstrates clearly an attempt to synthesise some elements to reflect the synoptic nature of the unit. There is a satisfactory awareness of change and/or continuity and/or development over the necessary extended period. The response reflects clear understanding of the question and a fair attempt to provide an appropriate argument supported by appropriate factual material. The approach mostly contains analysis or explanation but may lack balance and there may be some heavily descriptive/narrative passages and/or the answer may be somewhat lacking in appropriate supporting factual material. The answer is mostly relevant. The writing is generally fluent and the historical vocabulary is mostly appropriate. The grammar, punctuation and spelling are usually accurate.

Band IV: 30–35 marks

The answer demonstrates an uneven attempt to synthesise some elements to reflect the synoptic nature of the unit. There is an adequate awareness of change and/or continuity and/or development over the necessary extended period. The response indicates an attempt to argue relevantly, but the structure of the argument is poor. The approach depends more on heavily descriptive or narrative passages than on analysis or explanation (which may be limited to introductions and conclusions). Factual material, sometimes very full, is used to impart information or describe events rather than to address directly the requirements of the question. The writing may lack fluency and there may be some inappropriate historical vocabulary. The answer usually shows accuracy in grammar, punctuation and spelling but contains some careless errors.

Band V: 24–29 marks

The answer demonstrates a limited attempt to synthesise some elements to reflect the synoptic nature of the unit. There is a limited awareness of change and/or continuity and/or development over the necessary extended period. The response offers some elements of an appropriate answer but the approach lacks analysis or explanation and there is little attempt to link factual material to the requirements of the question. The structure of the answer shows weaknesses in organisation and the treatment of the topics is seriously unbalanced. The writing contains some inappropriate historical vocabulary. The answer shows some accuracy in grammar, punctuation and spelling but contains frequent errors.

Band VI: 12–23 marks

The answer demonstrates an unsatisfactory attempt to synthesise any elements and fails to reflect the synoptic nature of the module. There is no understanding of change and/or continuity and/or development over the necessary extended period. The answer is not focused on the requirements of the question and may be of very limited relevance. Any argument offered may be fragmentary and incoherent, and any assertions made may be unsupported by factual material. There may be serious irrelevance and/or serious weaknesses in knowledge. The writing shows significant weaknesses in the accuracy of grammar, punctuation and spelling.

Band VII: 0–11 marks

The answer demonstrates a totally unsatisfactory attempt to synthesise any elements and fails completely to reflect the synoptic nature of the unit. There is no understanding of change and/or continuity and/or development over the necessary extended period. There is no attempt to answer the question. There is no argument and no supporting evidence for any assertions. The answer is irrelevant and/or incoherent, perhaps in note form. The writing shows very major weakness in the accuracy of grammar, punctuation and spelling.

Note: candidates who do not address most of the 100-year period required by a question may not be put in band I for that essay.

Candidates who are overreliant on the insert and simply copy listed events should not receive a mark higher than the top of band V.

Using the generic mark scheme

Note the use of the word 'synthesise', which crops up in each of the bands. What this means is that essays should refer to examples from across the whole period in illustrating a particular point. The option has a natural dividing point — the change from tsarist autocracy to Bolshevik dictatorship in 1917 — but you must avoid the temptation simply to refer to the period of the tsars up to 1917 or to concentrate overwhelmingly on the post-1917 period. Incomplete essays of this kind would be unlikely to rise higher than band V or low band IV at best.

For example, imagine you are answering the question: 'How far were the Russian peasants continually exploited in the period 1855–1956?' You might begin by referring to the continued exploitation of the peasants after emancipation (e.g. lack of development of a *kulak* class, restrictive role of the *mir*, legally free but economically still enslaved). Then, you could go on to refer to the repressive activities of the land captains and the harsh treatments of the peasants during Witte's 'Great Spurt' of industrialisation in the 1890s (e.g. high taxation, lack of consumer goods, low prices for grain, rural overpopulation and land shortages). You could refer to the slight change of attitude under Stolypin and offer some judgement on the extent to which his policies succeeded or failed. You could then refer to the exploitation of the peasant-soldiers during the First World War and the harsh treatment of peasants during the Civil War and war communism. You should also consider the fate of the peasants under Stalin, during collectivisation and the liquidation of the *kulaks* as a class, making the point that there was a similarity in the way peasants were disregarded and exploited between the approaches of Witte and Stalin. You could then make the point that although Khrushchev did make some concessions to peasant interests, essentially the regime continued to treat the peasantry as objects.

Questions will often (but not always) begin with phrases such as 'How far?' or 'To what extent?' You must focus on these key phrases, and your conclusion must clearly show judgement on them. In the above example, for instance, the point could be made that whereas both the tsars and communists did have periods of 'relaxation' (emancipation, Stolypin, the NEP, Khrushchev), this was only to a limited extent and the overall theme of exploitation was common to both systems. Essays which fail to focus on the precise wording of the question are unlikely to rise above band IV.

The other important point to make about the mark scheme is that to go beyond the bottom of band III, essays *must* offer more than mere description or narrative. This is stated clearly in the requirements for bands I and II. Avoid simply offering a list of factors or aspects. Good candidates should constantly point out the similarities or differences between what happened under the tsars and the Bolsheviks.

Essays

It is essential that you spend up to 5 minutes in the exam on planning the basic structure of each essay. Do not launch straight into writing the essay. This tends to lead to narrative description and an overly chronological approach at the expense of focus and analysis. You should note elements of similarity/difference and change/continuity within the topic covered by the question. Often the wording of the question will dictate the approach, but you can either adopt a broadly chronological framework (as long as this doesn't simply lead to narrative) or structure the essay around similarities and then differences, coming to a balanced judgement in the conclusion.

As always, quality matters far more than quantity. You will have 45 minutes to write each essay in the exam. If allowance is made for 5 minutes of planning the essay, that leaves just 40 minutes. Examiners do not expect great quantities to be written during this time. Depending on the size of your handwriting, on average a good essay can be written on three to four sides of A4 paper. Indeed, many very good essays cover not much more than three sides. Do not use descriptive detail simply to 'pad out' the essay. A succinct and focused analysis is always better than long-winded description in which the argument is not always to the fore.

Content
Guidance

The main themes and developments in modern Russian history are covered in this section. For the sake of expediency, these themes are treated separately. However, there is an obvious linkage between themes, which you should bear in mind.

This section covers the following themes:
- Russian backwardness vis-à-vis the West
- Political culture
- Manifestations of autocracy
- Exploitation of the peasantry and industrial working classes

Within each of these themes, the major developments and key changes over the 100-year period are identified in broad detail. Aspects of continuity are considered as well as causes and consequences.

Words which are **emboldened** in the text are defined in glossaries at the end of each section.

Russian backwardness vis-à-vis the West

In 1931, developing remarks he had originally made at a meeting of the Central Committee of the Communist Party in 1928, Josef Stalin made arguably his most famous speech:

> Throughout history Russia has been beaten again and again because she was backward.... All have beaten her because of her military, industrial and agricultural backwardness. She was beaten because people have been able to get away with it. If you are backward and weak, then you are in the wrong and may be beaten and enslaved. But if you are powerful, people must beware of you.

> It is sometimes asked whether it is not possible to slow down industrialisation a bit. No, comrades, it is not possible! To slacken would mean falling behind. And those who fall behind get beaten.... That is why Lenin said during the October Revolution: 'Either perish, or overtake and outstrip the advanced capitalist countries.' We are 50 to 100 years behind the advanced countries. Either we make good the difference in 10 years or they crush us.

Stalin was touching on a fundamental and all-embracing theme in modern Russian history. When he made this speech, Russian agriculture was characterised by almost medieval modes of organisation and levels of technology and production. Industry was centred on a few industrial cities in the western part of the Soviet Union. The workforce was poorly educated and largely unskilled. Stalin's main purpose was to coerce party workers into renewed efforts in the forced modernisation programme, chiefly for defensive, military and 'great power' reasons.

Rulers of Russia from the eighteenth century onwards have always had pretensions to 'great power' status. Imperial Russia's claim to be one of the great powers appeared to be confirmed with the arrival of Alexander I's troops in Paris in 1814, which were instrumental in causing the fall of Napoleon I.

However, it was during the '30 wasted years' of the reign of Nicholas I (1825–55) that the widening gap in economic development between Russia and the West was accentuated. Britain was entering the secondary phase of industrialisation, as exemplified by the Great Exhibition of 1851. France under Napoleon III and Prussia during the 1850s were developing large-scale railway networks and forging ahead in coal and iron production. Nicholas I's Russia, meanwhile, impeded by the anti-industrialisation views of Finance Minister Egor Kankrin, had fallen far behind. This was shown by Russia's defeat in the Crimean War by Britain and France.

The Crimean War brought home to European statesmen and rulers a fundamental truth: great power status, and the related military capacity, depended increasingly on levels of industrialisation and modernisation. However, 'modernisation' was not sufficient in Russia's case. It was the need to 'catch up with the West' in industrial and agricultural technology and capacity which was the key requirement. This was the background, context and main purpose of the various reforms instigated by Alexander II, beginning with the emancipation of the serfs in 1861.

It was not just Lenin and Stalin in the twentieth century who referred to the need to catch up with the West. Many 'Westernisers' among the Russian intelligentsia, men like Alexander Herzen or the novelist Ivan Turgenev, travelled to western Europe and favourably compared its modern political systems, industry and agriculture with what they considered as the stagnant, often primitive, systems in Russia.

During the 1950s, after the death of Stalin, and during the height of the Cold War, Khrushchev's reforms in industry and agriculture, with an emphasis on production of more consumer goods, were undertaken as part of the need to catch up with the West. The same can be said of Gorbachev's programmes of *Glasnost* and *Perestroika* in the late 1980s.

Even during the post-Soviet era of the twenty-first century, visitors to Russia are struck by the comparative poverty and lack of variety of consumer goods and even, insofar as this can be discerned, comparatively low levels of military and industrial technology.

Causes of backwardness

In a major sense, there is one fundamental reason why it could be argued that Russia is unlikely ever to match, let alone overtake, the military and economic capacities of the more advanced Western countries. This is to do with the sheer size of Russia. The empire of the tsars stretched from Poland and the border with Imperial Germany in the west to the Bering Sea in the east. Under Khrushchev, the Soviet 'empire' stretched even further westwards to the border with West Germany. The 'empire' during the 100 years of this study occupied something like one-sixth of the world's land surface. It covered extremes of climate, from permafrost in the north near the Arctic Circle to sweltering heat in the south. It was often said that 'as the sun rises in the east of the empire, it is setting in the west'. The distance between St Petersburg, the capital of the tsarist empire, and New York is less than that between St Petersburg and Vladivostok in eastern Siberia.

In the introduction to his study of the 1917 revolution, Leon Trotsky wrote: 'Russia has been condemned by nature itself to a long backwardness.' Here he was making a link between Russia's size and its backwardness. Trotsky went on to point out, quite correctly, that no student can understand modern history fully without first appreciating the size of the country.

It is not that Russia lacked the resources for industrialisation in the nineteenth century. On the contrary, it possessed huge coal and oil reserves and potentially rich agricultural land in the Ukrainian 'breadbasket', and considerable mineral resources in the Caucasus mountains and Siberia. It was the difficulty of creating an effective communications system in such a vast empire that was the main problem. Without this, agricultural markets remained tiny and localised. Areas with food shortages could not be relieved effectively by transports from surplus areas, and vital raw material resources could not be connected to industrial areas easily.

It wasn't just size that had impeded Russian economic development. Within the ruling elite and government circles there were strong suspicions that industrialisation might bring undesirable social and political consequences. Moreover, Russia lacked a strong entrepreneurial spirit among its still small and undeveloped middle class. Serfdom, the basis and underpinning of Nicholas I's autocracy, prevented the development of free, mobile wage labour and a consumer market for the products of industry.

The result of all this was that by the time of Alexander II's accession in 1855 there was no clear governmental economic policy geared to progress and, compared with the West, Russia's economic development was slow. For example, only 4% of the world's cast iron and 2% of the world's steel were produced in Russia. Industrial workers formed only 0.75% of the total population of the empire, whereas 85% of the population were peasants working in agriculture. While there were some regional variations, on average only 5% of the population could be classed as literate.

Perhaps the most telling statistic concerns railway development. By 1900 railway development in Russia, as in most other continental countries, was to be the 'leading sector' in industrialisation. However, by 1855 there were only about 800 miles of railway in Russia. By comparison, the basis of Britain's modern railway network had been laid by the 1850s and the development of the French and Prussian/German rail networks was well under way. An often-quoted reason for Russia's defeat in the Crimea is that poorly equipped Russian troops had to be transported to the front by horse and cart along unmade dirt tracks.

Historians such as Hugh Seton-Watson and W. E. Mosse tend to agree that it was the emancipation of the serfs in 1861 that began the process of modernisation and industrialisation in Russia. However, it is clear that Russia started so far behind the West that the chances of catching up were very limited. Indeed, one major theme during the nineteenth and early twentieth centuries is that in many areas of industrial production and modernisation, the gap between Russia and countries like Germany and the USA was actually widening. This puts Stalin's remarks of 1931 into context, and helps to explain the drastic, dramatic nature of the forced industrialisation of Russia in the 1930s.

Economic development under the tsars

The reign of Alexander II

It is sometimes stated that there was very little economic progress under Alexander II. This is rather misleading. By 1881 the telegraph network in Russia had expanded to 50,000 miles, compared with 1,300 in 1855; there was 20 times as much railway mileage as in 1855; and there were five times as many joint-stock companies. The foundations of the great 'cradle' of the Russian coal and iron industry had been laid in the Donets Basin in the eastern Ukraine. Importantly, with the economic liberal Reutern as Minister of Finance from 1862 to 1878, there was a growing awareness of the need for the government to promote economic development actively. He improved and increased banking facilities and made large-scale loans more readily available to would-be industrialists. A firm basis for rapid economic development in the 1890s was laid during this period.

However, in absolute terms industrial progress was still very slow. By 1881 Russia still lagged far behind Britain, France and Germany in production of steel, coal and iron. Most serious of all was the comparative stagnation, indeed impoverishment in many areas, of Russian agriculture.

A fundamental aim of emancipation was to aid the development of free and mobile wage labour, encourage the large-scale development of an entrepreneurial **kulak** class and thereby encourage the growth of a large-scale mass consumer market to act as a stimulus and incentive for economic growth. In the main, with obvious regional variations and exceptions, this did not materialise. The unexpected **redemption payments** placed a heavy financial burden on the peasantry. The restrictive practices of the often conservative and reactionary **mir** as often as not acted as a disincentive to potentially enterprising peasants, by forbidding the cultivation of lucrative cash crops for industry like flax or hemp. Moreover, the revived tradition of rotating the land around the village on a tri-annual basis did little to encourage investment in the land. Local rules made it almost as difficult for peasants to leave their villages after 1861 as it had been under serfdom.

Perhaps most importantly, emancipation impeded the development of large-scale agriculture. In theory, ex-serfs were supposed to gain land holdings equivalent in size to those they had worked under serfdom. In practice, again with regional variations, the amount of land peasants gained was much smaller, particularly in the south of the empire.

What made this situation far worse was a near doubling of the peasant population in many parts of rural Russia during the second half of the nineteenth century. This was to have serious ramifications during the 1890s. By the time of Witte's 'Great Spurt' (see pp.17–18), Russian agriculture was still characterised by its small scale, a growing land shortage and 'land hunger', subsistence farming and periodic **'Malthusian' crises**. By 1881 there had clearly been no agricultural revolution such as that which had necessarily accompanied industrialisation in Britain. Many of the rural gentry were in debt and most peasants were impoverished. By the turn of the century more than half of the peasant farms were not even self-sufficient.

Thus, by the end of Alexander II's reign, despite some industrial and financial progress, Russia still lagged a long way behind the West, and in agriculture had fallen further behind the advanced agricultural economies of France, Germany, Britain and the USA.

Rapid industrialisation in the 1890s: Witte's 'Great Spurt'

In 1890, Bismarck, the Imperial German Chancellor who had sought desperately to maintain an alliance with Russia, was dismissed by the unstable new Kaiser William II, whose strong anti-Russian opinions were public knowledge. This, of course, was not the only reason for the rapid surge in industrialisation in Russia during the 1890s, but clearly the spectre of another conflict against a modern Western power was raised.

Sergei Witte was Minister of Finance from 1891 to 1903. He is usually given the credit for overseeing the rapid economic growth in Russia at the end of the century. In fact, he built on the work achieved by his two immediate predecessors, Bunge (1881–86) and Vyshnegradski (1886–91).

During the period 1880–1900, textile production doubled, petroleum production increased three and a half times, and coal production rose five-fold. While the value of imports remained steady (623 million roubles in 1880 as against 626 million in 1900), the value of exports rose dramatically (499 million roubles in 1880, 716 million in 1900).

The most dramatic indication of economic progress came in the form of railway development. In 1885, some 17,000 miles of track had been laid, rising to 40,000 by 1905. This clearly boosted the coal, iron and steel industries generally. In particular, vast spaces in the empire were linked — the Caspian and Black Seas, Moscow and the Ukraine — and, most dramatically, the Trans-Siberian railway was completed in 1905. This impressive project, begun in 1891, covered the almost 4,000 miles between Moscow and Vladivostok. Naturally the urban population increased considerably with the concentration of industrial workers into large-scale factories. By 1900 30% of factories employed more than 1,000 workers, and nearly half of all coal was produced from under 5% of coalmines. Cities like Odessa and Kiev doubled in population during the last decade of the nineteenth century.

These bare statistics suggest an impressive development. Undoubtedly Witte deserves his reputation as a forceful moderniser, not least because he demonstrated convincingly the need for scale and speed in catching up with the West and the need for the state to take a leading, guiding role. However, the social and political effects were less encouraging. The 'Great Spurt' was financed in the main by large-scale loans from Western countries, chiefly France, and the peasants were 'squeezed' not just by the existing redemption payments but by land taxes and high tariffs. As with Stalin in the 1930s, the Russian peasantry was exploited for supplies of grain to be exported to help pay for the necessary imports of capital and expertise from the West. This, it should be remembered, was forced upon a peasantry already largely impoverished after emancipation. Once again, the Russian peasantry was largely ignored as a potential consumer market. Moreover, the destabilising effect of rapid urbanisation, with the creation of a half-peasant, half-worker 'class', could have political implications.

The situation in 1914

It is estimated that by 1914 the tsarist empire had the world's fifth largest industrial capacity, an impressive rate of development when compared with the 1860s. In one sense, clearly, Russia's very backward starting point had some advantages, as the most modern technology and expertise imported from the West could be used. Overall, the annual increase in Russia's industrial productivity averaged just under 6% (compared with just over 5% for the USA, 4.5% for Germany and only 2% for Britain). However, Russia's reputation as the world's fastest-growing economy at this time does create a slightly misleading impression. In many sectors, the gap between Russia and the more advanced Western economies was as wide as ever, if not widening even further. For example, in the production of iron, Russia was still behind Britain and Germany and far behind the USA. Russia was producing only about one-fifth of Germany's output of steel. It still lagged behind even the less advanced Balkan countries in the amount of land covered by railways (although this was largely because of the sheer size of its empire).

This gap can be explained partly by the effects of the worldwide recession on the Russian economy after 1900, and the effects of the Russo–Japanese War and the 1905 revolution, all of which interrupted and partially ruined the impressive growth rates in the coal and oil industries in the Donets Basin and the Caucasus.

It was in agriculture that the widening gap between Russia and the West was most pronounced. While the USA, Britain, Germany and to some extent France were moving towards a more modern, capital-intensive, larger-scale farming industry, Russian agriculture was still small scale and labour intensive. In 1914 80% of the population was employed in some way in agricultural pursuits, compared with around 10% in Britain and around 40% in Germany. On the eve of the Great War, Russia was still essentially a poor, peasant country with a per capita income estimated at no more than 30% of the Western average.

The agricultural reforms of the other great 'modernising' statesman of this period, Peter Stolypin, had been aimed at creating a *kulak* class of prosperous peasants (for political as well as economic reasons). This 'wager on the strong', a deliberate piece of social engineering, was a belated attempt to create an inviting domestic consumer market for the products of industry and to increase grain production for export. It was also an attempt to rectify the neglect of the peasantry by Witte, and can be seen as a telling comment on the failings of Alexander II's emancipation of 1861, as suggested by Stolypin's almost panic-stricken plea: 'Give us 20 more years and we will be safe.'

The abolition of redemption payments, the establishment of facilities for cheap loans and encouragement of peasants to break free from the *mir* had only partial success. Stolypin was assassinated in 1911 and his reforms were interrupted by war in 1914, but it is estimated that by 1916 only 20% of the Russian peasantry had taken advantage of the reforms. More tellingly, the figures for those leaving the *mir* were actually declining after an initial spurt from 1908 to 1910. This suggests one important reason for the continued backwardness and poverty of Russian agriculture: the majority of Russian peasants lacked any kind of entrepreneurial spirit. Stolypin was, after all, asking the peasants to branch out on their own, to take risks. It seems that the majority preferred the security provided by the restrictive practices of the *mir*.

By 1914 Russia had made some impressive progress towards modernisation — the fundamental objective of Alexander II's reforms begun in 1861. However, the reigns of the last three tsars of Russia began with defeat in one war against the West and ended with another, in 1917. The real test of the success or failure of Alexander II's modernisation would come when Russia again found itself involved in military conflict with a major Western power. That, of course, came in 1914, when Russia found itself at war with Imperial Germany, the most modernised, well-equipped and well-trained military power in Europe. It was here that Russia's comparative economic and industrial backwardness was to prove crucial.

The impact of war in the 1920s

Clearly, Russia was in no state to wage the first 'total war' in history. Stories of poorly-equipped and poorly-led Russian peasant-soldiers being slaughtered on the eastern front are legendary. Russian industry was unable to supply weapons, uniforms and ammunition in anything like sufficient quantity. Wagon loads of grain were left to rot in railway sidings in the provinces for want of locomotive pulling power. The necessary militarisation of transport led to worsening food shortages in major cities like Petrograd and Moscow, which were a vital contributor to the fall of the tsar in February 1917. The devastation caused to the Russian economy by war, accentuated by the loss of vast areas of industrial and agricultural land in the Treaty of Brest-Litovsk in 1918, was made even worse by the ravages of the Civil War between 1918 and 1921.

The immediate economic priority of the new Bolshevik government was to generate sufficient industrial and agricultural production to enable it to defeat the various 'White' armies attempting to remove the Bolshevik 'Reds' and cling to power. Longer-term economic goals at this stage were of necessity given a lower priority. 'War communism', that curious mixture of ideology and pragmatism, was to have an adverse effect on industrial and agricultural productivity.

Of course, at the outset the new Bolshevik government implemented schemes for a future planned 'command economy'. In 1918, within months of the seizure of power, the new government established the Supreme Council of the National Economy (*Vesenkha*). This was the central driving force of war communism, and very soon most large industrial enterprises had come under the control of the state, most private enterprise and trade was suppressed, and the labour force was controlled directly from the centre.

This was followed in 1921 by the establishment of the State Planning Commission (*Gosplan*). There were attempts to introduce cooperative, 'collectivised' forms of farming, although many of these were to be short-lived. More importantly, because of the urgent need to feed and supply the Red Army and the urban population, notorious 'grain requisition squads' were sent to the countryside to procure (in effect, steal) large quantities of grain from peasant villages. The extremely harsh punishments handed out to hoarders of grain and the obvious lack of incentive for peasant grain producers led to dramatic decreases in the amount of grain sown, leading to the first great rural tragedy under the Bolsheviks: the great famine of 1921–22, in which an estimated 5 million people died.

By the time the Reds had won the Civil War in 1921, industrial productivity had fallen to about 15% of its pre-1914 level. The major textile and metallurgical centres were particularly badly affected. The picture in agriculture was no better, with less than 70% of land being farmed compared with 1914. Growing incidences of peasant insurrections, particularly in Tambov Province, worker unrest, and ultimately the rebellion at Kronstadt of the 'Red sailors' formed the backdrop to the decision at the Tenth Party Congress to adopt Lenin's New Economic Policy.

The New Economic Policy (NEP)

The NEP, described famously by Lenin as 'Two steps forwards, one step back', had two fundamental aims. The first, an urgent political aim, was to recapture support from the disaffected peasantry by allowing some measure of private enterprise in farming (after compulsory quotas of produce had been supplied to the state), and gain support from the workers by allowing a partial return to capitalism for enterprises employing ten workers or fewer. The second important aim was to allow a breathing space for Russia, to regain the 1913 levels of agricultural and industrial production as soon as possible.

Lenin justified what in some party quarters was seen as a heresy by reiterating the same argument he had employed on the eve of the Bolshevik **coup** and on the signing of the Treaty of Brest-Litovsk: that the impending Bolshevik-style revolutions in the industrially advanced West, in particular in Germany, would enable Russia to modernise more quickly on genuine socialist lines. In any case, the state would retain control of big enterprises, the 'commanding heights' of the economy. Moreover, during this 'breathing space', the backward population would be educated in socialist, collective forms of agricultural and industrial production; and there would be vast literacy and propaganda campaigns which would not only make the link (*smychka*) in people's minds between the worker and the peasant, the hammer and the sickle, but importantly the link between socialism and modernisation ('communism equals Soviet power plus electrification').

If judged by the rationale with which Lenin introduced the policy in 1921, the NEP can be deemed to have been a success. Most economic historians agree that by 1926 Russia had indeed recovered its 1913 levels of production in many areas of industry and agriculture and that most peasants and workers were considerably more content in the freer atmosphere of the NEP than under war communism. However, in a much more important sense the NEP was a failure because under it, Russia had fallen even further behind the West. The USA was prospering during the boom years of the 'Roaring Twenties', Weimar Germany was benefiting from vast loans under the Dawes Plan, and Japan's military-industrial complex was developing rapidly. Meanwhile, Russia's industry remained under-financed and technologically backward and its agriculture, based on production from 25.5 million small-scale farms, remained stuck in a medieval time warp.

After Lenin

By the time Lenin died in 1924 the expected socialist-style revolutions in more advanced countries like Germany, France and Britain had either not materialised or failed. This meant that by 1925, Soviet, socialist Russia was alone and isolated in a potentially hostile capitalist world. Moreover, if one takes Japan to be a part of the infinitely more advanced West, Russia was encircled by potential enemies. The experience of the Civil War, when Western countries had sent armies to help the Whites' attempt to overthrow the Bolsheviks, had brought home to Bolshevik party leaders the vulnerability of Soviet Russia. Moreover, it was very distasteful for Bolshevik leaders to have to accept that much of Russia's industrial production was in the hands of 'petty capitalists' and, even more worryingly, that the hugely important agricultural sector was being led by the hated class enemy, the *kulaks*.

The growing awareness within the higher ranks of the party leadership of the need for greatly accelerated agricultural and industrial productivity to catch up with the capitalist West formed the backdrop to the dramatic struggles for the leadership after 1924 between Stalin, Trotsky, Zinoviev, Kamenev and Bukharin. It was not that party leaders disagreed on the need for rapid modernisation; it was the *methods* that divided them. The fundamental question initially was the extent to which the NEP should be exploited and manipulated by the party. As it stood, the NEP simply could not provide the structural framework for the necessary large-scale and rapid modernisation. This was fraught with political difficulties. If the peasants were to be 'squeezed' by raising grain quotas (as advocated at varying times by Trotsky, Zinoviev, Kamenev and even Bukharin), might this not cause a return of peasant hostility, similar to that of the war communism period? The idea that Lenin's NEP should be abandoned so quickly and replaced by a system even harsher than that of war communism was unthinkable.

The Stalin faction's adoption of the propaganda slogan 'socialism in one country' was, of course, an abandonment of Marxist internationalist principles since it meant that Soviet Russia was to turn its back on the rest of the world. However, this was a practical acceptance of the realities of the situation during the late 1920s, as Trotsky's (and Lenin's) 'Permanent Revolution' was now obsolete and irrelevant. It can be argued that it was the failure of Lenin's expected revolutions in the more advanced countries that led to the drastic Stalin solution of the 1930s. By 1928–29, as under Alexander II and under Witte, Russia had to modernise rapidly, not just for the traditional 'great power' reasons, but more urgently for military-defensive reasons, since it had fallen so far behind the West. By that time, the real struggle had boiled down to that between Bukharin's urging of a stricter manipulation of the NEP 'at a snail's pace' and the instigation of a vastly more direct forcing of economic development, a policy that would inevitably bring great human hardship. By the time Stalin had effectively won the struggle for power in 1929, Russia had as its dictator a man sufficiently brutal, single-minded and fanatical to launch such a policy.

The Stalin solution of the 1930s

Arguably, the 1930s has been the most written-about period in modern Russian history. The debate has usually centred on the question: 'Was Stalin really necessary?' This is the title of a work published by the economic historian Alec Nove. Even after Khrushchev's notorious 'De-Stalinisation' speech of 1956, Soviet apologists continued to argue that Stalin was indeed 'necessary'. In the post-Soviet era far fewer historians are willing to argue this. This is not the place to comment on the rights and wrongs of Stalin's policies, but rather to highlight the fact that Stalin faced the same dilemma as his autocratic predecessors: the need to modernise Russia rapidly and to catch up with the West.

'Stalinism' has come to mean rule by terror and force, the brutal imposition of forced labour camps, the murder of all those in a position to challenge for power, the 'liquidation' of an entire class of the peasantry (the *kulaks*), the innovation of a planned, forced command economy, directed and controlled almost totally by the state, and the brutal instigation of totalitarian rule. It is sometimes easy to forget that the brutal aspects of the regime, the purges and the Terror need to be put into the context of what Stalin was attempting to achieve: the compression into 10 years of a process that in liberal Britain took more than a century and in France effectively a century and a half to achieve.

Stalin's fundamental aim was to catch up with the West with a programme of forced, rapid industrialisation, but there were more immediate practical advantages: the institution of a command economy would enable the state to control and dictate every aspect of economic growth, from setting targets and quotas for production to controlling and regulating the labour supply. The state would act as director, producer and consumer. With the state having executive power over the economy, the use of force and terror would enable a rapid economic development which the liberal, free-market systems of Britain and France clearly could not have achieved.

The collectivisation of agriculture

The collectivisation of agriculture would solve a number of problems at once: the state would, to a large extent, be able to dictate agricultural as well as industrial production. Just as importantly, it would be able to dictate and control the requisition of grain in a way unthinkable under the NEP and very difficult to achieve under war communism. It would, at long last, remove the Bolshevik state's dependence on the class enemy, the *kulaks*. Agricultural output would no longer be governed by the vicissitudes of the free market. The dismantling of millions of small private farms and their replacement with giant large-scale collectives would facilitate the introduction of modern technology — the tractors and combine harvesters produced in the Five Year Plans.

Crucially, the agricultural sector could be forced to produce and supply the vast quantities of grain needed as exports to pay for the necessary imports of technology and expertise and to feed the growing urban population. The whole programme of 'co-operative', collective farming (as with the Five Year Plans) could be presented in propaganda terms as part of Bolshevik, socialist ideology — although the forced collectivisation of agriculture had little to do with genuine Marxist doctrine.

Collectivisation would inevitably cause considerable human suffering, but this was considered to be of secondary importance. As was the case with Witte's policies in the 1890s, the agricultural sector and the Russian peasantry would have to pay for rapid industrialisation. The idea of exploiting the peasantry for the benefit of the state was nothing new in modern Russian history, although the methods and scale of exploitation under Stalin would be of a kind not seen previously. In official propaganda, it would not be the peasants who would suffer (on the contrary, they would benefit), but the dehumanised class enemy, the *kulaks*, who had to be 'liquidated as a class'.

The Five Year Plans

As had been the situation with Witte's policies, the Five Year Plans would inevitably have to focus on heavy 'producer goods' industries, and this was certainly the case with the first two plans. The third Five Year Plan did originally make some allowance for more consumer goods, but with the outbreak of war in 1939 this was abandoned in favour of tank and aircraft production.

Under Stalin, as with Witte, Russia was still in the primary stage of industrialisation, and this was accentuated by a low starting point and the growing need (particularly after the coming to power of Hitler in 1933) to catch up rapidly. It is in this primary stage, with the inevitable concentration on items such as coal, iron, steel, oil, the construction of dams and canals and so on, that the benefits to the state far outweigh those to the individual. The first two Five Year Plans would be foreshortened and the quotas and targets constantly revised upwards. Inevitably, there would be criticisms and complaints, not just about the human suffering involved, but also about the poor quality of much of what was produced. Complaints could not be tolerated, and the use of scapegoats through the purges, portraying the accused as 'saboteurs', and the introduction of forced labour camps in the *gulag*, were important aspects of the modernisation programme. As suggested previously, the brutal aspects of the regime, the Terror, should not be considered in isolation. They were an integral part of Stalin's 'revolution from above'.

To what extent did Russia catch up with the West in the 1930s?

This is difficult to assess. Some of the Soviet industrial and agricultural statistics are questionable, and the answer depends on which perspective one takes. It is the subject of historical debate, bound up as it is with the question of whether Stalinism was really 'necessary'.

There is no doubt that the tanks and aircraft produced in the Five Year Plans enabled Soviet Russia to win the war on the eastern front by 1945. It is also true that after 1945 the Soviet Union was a world superpower. Russia's status as a major power was greater than at any time in its history. Moreover, the impressive production figures of the 1930s were achieved at a time when the capitalist West was in the crisis of the Depression.

Industry

Taken at face value, the statistics for production in the main heavy industries look impressive: between 1928 (the last effective year of the NEP) and 1940, the output of coal rose from 35 million to 150 million tons, steel from 3 million to 18 million, and oil from 12 million to 26 million. By 1940, at a time when the USA's share of world manufacturing output had fallen to under 30%, Russia's had risen to just under 20%, surpassing Britain (9%) and Germany (13%). In this sense, Russia was catching up with, and indeed surpassing, most of the West and can be seen to have had even the USA in its sights.

These statistics should be qualified by two factors: one is the poor quality of much that was produced in the Five Year Plans (especially steel and iron) and the other is that, if one excludes Nazi Germany, the capitalist economies of the West had yet to recover fully from the effects of the Depression. There is no doubt, however, that these growth rates far exceeded anything that had previously been achieved in the Russian economy. During this period, the urban population rose from around 25 million to 55 million and the industrial workforce again more than doubled from 11 million to over 23 million. The infrastructure of a modern industrial economy had been created. Magnitogorsk in the Ural mountains, the great propaganda showpiece of the regime, was the centre of a giant metallurgical complex. Whole new industrial conurbations had been created in Siberia (the Kuznetsk Basin) and along the river Dnieper with its dams and hydroelectric power stations. Huge canals had been constructed, linking some of the major rivers. To help modernise agriculture, between 1928 and 1940 the manufacture of fertilisers rose from 0.1 million to over 3 million tons, whilst the number of tractors manufactured increased from 1,300 to over 31,000.

However, it is quite likely that Stalin exaggerated the low level of industrial output and development in 1928 (although the fundamental point about Russia lagging far behind the West was still true). It has also been argued by some historians that the impressive growth rates achieved between 1890 and 1914, had they not been interrupted by war, civil war and the revolutions of 1917, would have achieved production levels not unlike those achieved at such huge cost by Stalin. However, to indulge in speculation of this kind does not take us very far. The plain fact is that in many senses, Stalin's modernisation of industry enabled Russia to take great strides in catching up with the West.

Agriculture

In agriculture, the picture was not so impressive. It has often been said that it was not until well into the 1950s and the Khrushchev era that Russian agriculture recovered from the ravages of collectivisation. Even in the 1950s Russian agriculture remained technologically under-equipped and hugely labour-intensive, compared with the large-scale capital-intensive farming of, for example, Canada and the USA. Collectivisation had deprived agriculture of its hardest-working and most energetic and productive farmers — the *kulaks*. The incentive to produce for one's own profit had been lost and was not compensated for by the introduction of the small private plots instigated after Stalin's 'dizzy with success' speech. *Kulaks* in their thousands destroyed valuable livestock rather than turn it over to the collective. Between 1928 and 1932 alone, the estimated number of horses fell from 33 million to just over 15 million, of cattle from 70 million to 35 million, sheep from over 140 million to 42 million, and pigs from 26 million to under 9 million.

The immediate consequence of this was the largest famine to date in Russian history. Between 7 million and 10 million people died of starvation in 1932, prompting the suicide of Stalin's wife and growing criticism from party leaders in the *Politburo*, such as Kirov. Stalin's refusal to reduce grain requisitions for export in order to ease the famine (indeed, there is evidence that he actually increased them) meant that there were severe food shortages until 1939. At no time during the 1930s was there a food surplus, and by the time of the Nazi invasion of the Soviet Union in 1941 Russian agriculture was still unable to feed its population adequately. The area affected most drastically by collectivisation was the traditional 'breadbasket' of the Ukraine. The fact that, initially, thousands of Ukrainian peasants welcomed the invading Nazi hordes in 1941 is a telling comment on the whole collectivisation programme, as is the fact that by the outbreak of the Second World War, Russian agricultural productivity had only just recovered to the levels of 1914.

Conclusion

The main criticism of Stalin's modernisation policies concerns their largely short-term nature. As has been pointed out, Russia was able to make strides in catching up with the West chiefly because of the Depression, but this was inherently a temporary and cyclical phenomenon. During the years after 1945, most Western capitalist economies were able to recover and resume economic progress at a far greater rate than the USSR. The huge and growing gap between levels of productivity for both producer and consumer goods, and in living standards generally, was most notable in comparing the US and Soviet economies, but there were equally notable comparisons with France (which was undergoing an industrial 'take-off'), West Germany and Japan.

Stalin had effectively produced a one-dimensional and unbalanced economy, overreliant on heavy goods industries and on force and coercion rather than encouragement and incentives. This was sufficient to produce impressive short-term gains and, importantly, to enable the USSR to win the war against Hitler. In the longer term, however, Stalin bequeathed his eventual successor, Khrushchev, a straitjacketed economic system with little or no flexibility, which had neglected the peasantry, was unable to provide decent living standards, and had underinvested drastically in agriculture. It is often said that Stalin 'dragged Russia kicking and screaming into the twentieth century'. However, by the time of his death in 1953, in many important aspects Russia was as far behind the West as ever.

Postscript: 1956

There is no doubt that by 1956 Khrushchev, who had won the struggle to succeed Stalin, was well aware that in many key areas Russia continued to lag behind the West. He made genuine attempts to close the gap, in particular to catch up in living standards and provision of foodstuffs and consumer goods. His fundamental aim was to demonstrate that the Soviet way of life, measured by living standards, was superior to that of the West. This was to be the vital underpinning of the policy of 'peaceful coexistence'. Many of his policies (later dismissed by his rivals and critics as 'harebrained schemes') were geared to this end. He attempted to overtake Western agricultural productivity by restoring the place of agriculture in the economy. His 'Virgin Lands Campaign', started in 1954, aimed to develop under-cultivated lands in Kazakhstan and parts of Siberia for crop farming. He attempted to provide more local incentives and individual initiatives. He relaxed some of the strict controls over the collective farms, raised prices paid to peasants for foodstuffs, and gave a higher profile to the small private plots on the collective farms.

However, the Virgin Lands Campaign was poorly implemented. Little attention was paid to matters of climate and local conditions. Overreliance on the production of maize and under-provision of fertilisers were also part of the problem. While Russian and Soviet grain production figures in the 1950s were more impressive than in the 1930s, the setbacks to agriculture caused by the policies of the 1930s were an insurmountable hurdle. The fact that in 1963, despite undoubted improvements in agricultural productivity, the USSR had to import large quantities of grain, mainly from North America, to avert yet another famine shows just how far Russia remained behind the West in agriculture.

In industry, too, Khrushchev made genuine attempts to re-balance the economy by providing more consumer goods. He allowed some relaxation of the controls of the

Five Year Plans. Material rewards and incentives were increased, and there was some attempt to decentralise aspects of the command economy by giving more local initiatives.

Khrushchev's problem was that he was trying to redress the faults of a rigid planning system that had been in place for a quarter of a century. He was impeded by the inherent conservatism of Stalinist economic planners, and he was severely restricted in the desire to produce more consumer goods by the demands of heavy industry at the height of the Cold War. While it is true that for a short time in the 1950s the USSR overtook the USA in the space race, the Russian way of life continued to be characterised by long queues and waiting lists, shortages of food and housing, limited quality, quantity and choice of consumer goods and dire poverty, particularly among the peasantry. In this respect, despite advances made under Witte and Stalin, little had changed, and in many important areas, Russia remained a long way behind the West.

Glossary

kulak: 'rich' peasant

redemption payment: payment made by peasants for their freedom following the Emancipation of the Serfs (1861)

mir: traditional village commune

'Malthusian' crises: periodic crises where population growth exceeds the ability of agriculture to supply the necessary food

coup: political takeover

gulag: Soviet concentration camp system set up in 1930

Political culture

In 1917, days after the fall of the Romanov dynasty, Lenin was making arrangements to hurry back to Russia. 'Russia is now the freest country in the world,' he said. The Provisional Government, led by Kadets, Octobrists and middle-class liberals, aimed eventually to establish a liberal, democratic, republican system of government. There would be a **Constituent Assembly**, a multiparty political system, universal male suffrage and more freedoms of press and worship than had ever existed under the tsars. The Provisional Government consisted of the core of deputies elected to the fourth Duma in 1912. It would at last provide Russia with the civil liberties and democratic freedoms that had long been enjoyed in France, the USA and Britain and had been denied by Nicholas II's Fundamental Laws of 1906. However, as it transpired, the Provisional Government from February to October was to be only a brief interlude in the usually autocratic nature of government in Russia.

Within months, at the Second All-Russian Congress of Soviets on 28 October 1917, Lenin and the Bolsheviks proclaimed power in Russia. Elections to the proposed Constituent Assembly went ahead, but in January 1918, when deputies from the Kadet,

Menshevik, Socialist Revolutionary (SR), Left Social Revolutionary and Bolshevik parties went to the assembly building in the capital to begin the second day's session, they found Red Guards at the gate and notices proclaiming that the assembly was to be abolished.

The Bolsheviks were nominally in a loose coalition with Left SRs. However, they were already ruling as a single party and this was confirmed by the outbreak of civil war in the summer of 1918. Thus, within the space of just a few months, Russia went from one form of autocracy to another. Genuine democracy lasted for the 24 hours of the first session of the Constituent Assembly. Russia would have to wait until 1991–92 for the beginnings of anything resembling genuine democratic freedom.

What is particularly interesting and significant about the forced closure of the Constituent Assembly in January 1918 is that there were only a few brief and sporadic protests against the abandonment of the democratic experiment, and these were dealt with easily by the Red Guards. There are a number of short-term and immediate reasons for the failure of the Provisional Government. A fundamental reason was the fateful decision of the Foreign Minister, Miliukov, to continue Russia's involvement in the war, which among other things meant delaying important measures such as dealing with the land question, workers' rights, and legitimisation of the government by holding immediate elections. The government also faced an important rival power bloc in the form of the Petrograd and Moscow soviets.

These are very important reasons for the failure of the democratic experiment, but the root cause is that the members of the Provisional Government (academics, members of the professional classes, businessmen and industrialists) were essentially operating in a vacuum. There was no genuine liberal-democratic tradition in Russian political culture, or at least such a tradition was very weak. Russian middle-class liberals were unrepresentative and had a narrow and weak basis of support. In part this was a consequence of Russia's continuing economic and social backwardness, with its inevitably small middle class lacking in genuine independence. This explains why many historians claim that real power after the fall of Nicholas II lay with the soviets — elected councils of peasants, soldiers and workers' deputies. Russian politics had become extremely polarised under the last three tsars. Tsarist autocracy was now thoroughly discredited by associations with Rasputin and disasters in war; Russian generals (despite Kornilov's attempt) were unable to impose military dictatorship because of urgent matters on the eastern front; the middle-class Provisional Government was unable to exert effective control; and 'power lay on the streets', as Lenin's famous remark put it.

The essential point is that from the nineteenth century, and even more so after 1917, Russian political culture was autocratic, authoritarian and therefore fundamentally anti-liberal. Tsarist autocracy, with its ideology of 'Orthodoxy, Autocracy, Nationality', underpinned by the Russian Orthodox Church, was eventually replaced by the equally autocratic ideology of Marxism-Leninism-Stalinism.

Accidents of geography and history can go some way towards explaining the development of an autocratic and authoritarian political culture. The sheer size of the empire, with its numerous nationalities, religions, local traditions and cultures, variations of climate and poor communications, made the task of ruling very difficult. The tsar-autocrat was not known as the 'tsar of Russia' but as the 'tsar of *all* the Russias'. Ruling over and defending this empire required strong government. Some form of autocratic, authoritarian system can be seen to be more appropriate than any form of representative government. Moreover, representative government would surely require a measure of literacy and education which was restricted to a tiny minority during the nineteenth century.

In a different sense the same point can be made about Bolshevik Russia. What had been the tsarist empire became the Soviet empire. The new government's most urgent and pressing task was to cling onto power at all costs, defend the Soviet Union and extend and impart its ideology throughout the disparate empire.

The weakness of the liberal tradition

There is a close correlation between geography, size, economic and social backwardness and the weakness of a liberal tradition. In the words of the American sociologist Barrington Moore Jnr, 'no bourgeois...no democracy'. Liberal democracy in the French or American forms, which the Provisional Government had hoped to emulate, had developed in the West alongside the growth and development of a numerous, strong and essentially independent middle class. In Britain, France and the USA such a development stretched back to the eighteenth century — in England's case, arguably to the sixteenth century. If the experiment in liberal democracy failed dramatically in the comparatively advanced German Confederation during the revolutions of 1848, then, bearing in mind the social composition of the Russian population throughout most of the nineteenth and early twentieth centuries — a small aristocratic elite, a vast, largely illiterate peasantry, a small but developing industrial working class and a tiny middle-class intelligentsia — the chances for a sufficiently strong middle class (the essential underpinning of liberalism) in Russia were small indeed.

Another important reason for the lack of development of a strong liberal tradition is the general polarisation of Russian politics throughout the second half of the nineteenth century. Between the reforms of Alexander II in the 1860s and the institution of the Imperial State Duma under Nicholas II in 1906, there had been a developing cycle of repression and reaction on the one hand and growing revolutionary violence on the other. This characterises the development of Russian politics and, crucially, it meant that Russian political development was *revolutionary* rather than *evolutionary*. The chance, therefore, of a relatively peaceful 'middle way' developing in Russian politics receded with every decade.

It could be said that the liberal middle way should have developed from the 1860s; Alexander II should have laid the basis for the establishment of an elected national parliament — a state Duma. He adopted Western measures with the establishment of *zemstva* — locally elected councils for local government — and he borrowed from Western models for his legal reforms. Had a parliamentary tradition been established by the 1870s this would have provided a legal and comparatively peaceful forum for opposition to the tsar's policies. Gradually, by the turn of the century, the tsar could have become a genuine constitutional monarch, liberal democracy could have taken root, and Russia's political development would not have taken the violent revolutionary turn it did.

As it was, when Alexander II belatedly flirted with the beginnings of a representative legislative system (the Loris-Melikov proposals of 1880–81) it was already too late to establish the middle way. The assassination of Alexander II in 1881 led to the suppression of anti-autocratic forces by Alexander III and Pobedonostsev.

By the time Nicholas II reluctantly issued the October Manifesto in the chaos of revolution in 1905, it was certainly too late. In any case, the granting of a state Duma for the first time in Russian history was only intended to overcome a dangerous revolutionary situation in the autumn of 1905. When the heat and dust of revolution had settled in 1906 and the uprising was suppressed, the tsar showed his true colours with the Fundamental Laws, which gave virtually no real power to the elected assembly.

The Russia of 1906–14 was certainly not a constitutional monarchy in any meaningful sense. The fourth Duma of 1912 had not won any significant political concessions other than those few granted to the first Duma of 1906. This unwillingness to grant political concessions and incorporate Duma liberals into political decision making continued into the war, and led to the development of the Progressive Bloc in 1915.

According to this argument, the problems all date back to the 1860s. Alexander II simply did not go far enough. A vital opportunity was missed and any subsequent attempts to establish some form of representative political system fell victim to the polarisation of Russian politics, which eventually was to render the experiment of the Provisional Government in 1917 futile.

This whole argument offers a helpful explanation of the development of Russian politics in the late nineteenth and early twentieth centuries. However, it is based on a false assumption — that Alexander II was ever likely to be willing to grant a national, elected representative assembly. He was a genuine autocrat and, while he was prepared to listen to the 'Westernisers' to an extent in his reforms, the concept of parliamentary liberalism (like revolutionary Marxism later on) was alien to him. Alexander II had been brought up by his father to be an autocrat, just as he brought up his own son Alexander III, and he in turn brought up his son Nicholas II. If Alexander II can be thought of as the 'tsar-liberator' at all, it can only be in a narrow, Russian sense.

All this is not, of course, to deny the existence of liberalism as a force in Russian politics. On the contrary, by 1900 there was a lively liberal movement which advocated representative assemblies, freedom of speech and opinion, and generally the civil liberties enjoyed by many of those in the West. However, for the reasons given earlier, it operated within very narrow confines.

The development of tsarist autocracy

The nature and meaning of tsarist autocracy

It is outside the scope of this guide to trace the development of tsarist autocracy to its sixteenth-century roots. However, Nicholas I's Education Minister Uvarov summed up the basis of Russian autocracy as 'Orthodoxy, Autocracy and Nationality'. This slogan, which might seem to be an early nineteenth-century 'soundbite', in effect became the vital underpinning of autocracy. 'Autocracy' can be defined as a system of government where the powers of the monarch are legally unrestricted. Russian autocracy was a far purer form of individual rule than, say, the absolute monarchy by divine right of Louis XIV in France. The French absolute monarchs, like their Russian counterparts, relied on the support of organised religion. The difference was that the absolute monarch in Catholic countries in the West had to contend with the fact that ultimate power over the Catholic Church was in the hands of the Pope in Rome. In Russia, by contrast, ruling through the Procurator (head) of the Holy Synod, the tsar-autocrat was in ultimate control of the Russian Orthodox Church.

It is important to remember that the tsar-autocrat had duties as well as privileges and rights. These were above all the duty of defending the empire against foreign attacks and overseeing the general welfare of its peoples. While it could be argued that this latter duty was largely neglected, particularly by Nicholas II, the duty of defending the empire was taken very seriously.

Until 1906, there was no effective constitutional form of representation in Russia. There were no elected national assemblies. The laws of the land, the hiring and firing of government ministers, and the direction of government policies in all respects were in the hands of the tsar-autocrat. There was an important body of advisers and ministerial experts, but the Council of State, an often large and unwieldy affair, was subordinated wholly to the tsar. A vast and even more unwieldy bureaucracy was essential to administer such an extensive empire.

At the highest level, the senior civil servants were very important, often able and privileged men enjoying the higher ranks and status in Russian society. Tolstoy's fictional Karenin, in his novel *Anna Karenina*, is a good example. Within these senior ranks there was rarely a uniformity of views and opinions. As with the Council of State, there were differences between those who might be called the 'progressives' (who can largely be said to have had the upper hand in the 1860s) and the 'obscurantists' or reactionaries, who had far more influence in the 1870s and under Alexander III. At the lower end, chiefly in the provinces, were the minor bureaucrats, usually men of poor education and low ability. Such men were often paid low wages and were therefore open to bribery and corruption. A good portrait of the poorly paid functionary is provided in Gogol's play *The Government Inspector*.

A paternalistic system

Russian autocracy could therefore best be described as a **paternalistic** system of government. The tsar-autocrat was the patriarch. It is important to emphasise that Alexander II and Alexander III had been taught as heirs to the imperial throne to do their duty. They were taught that they were responsible to God and in a sense that they were the Almighty's representative on earth. The tsar-autocrat therefore was the father of his peoples. Just as God was 'our father in heaven', so the tsar was 'our father on earth'. This was clearly a highly personal form of monarchy. Indeed, the tsars were often referred to as 'our father' or 'our little father' by the peasantry. In the years immediately preceding and following the emancipation of the serfs in 1861, Alexander II was commonly referred to as 'our father the tsar-liberator'. In January 1905, on the day of Bloody Sunday, Father Gapon began the petition he hoped to present to Nicholas II by referring to 'our tsar, the father of our peoples'. In 1913, on his tour of western parts of the empire, commemorating 300 years of Romanov rule, Nicholas II was met everywhere he went in provincial Russia with icons portraying him as 'our father'. Most significantly, the same reaction was manifested in August 1914 when he blessed the (largely peasant-based) troops on their way to the eastern front.

These last two examples serve to illustrate the perception of tsarist autocracy as a popular form of monarchy. In a system which invested such vast powers in the hands of one man, this had its advantages. When the peasantry felt disillusioned with various governmental policies, it wasn't the tsar himself who was held to be to blame, but his 'evil' ministers. The hundreds of peasant riots and disturbances which broke out after the disappointing terms of emancipation became known were focused not on the 'tsar-liberator' himself but on his advisers, who were thought to have distorted and wrongly implemented his policies. The point of Father Gapon's petition on Bloody Sunday was to bring to Nicholas's attention some of the bad things that were going on in his name. Those peasants who prostrated themselves in front of the royal personage in 1913 and 1914 would not think of blaming Nicholas for their many grievances — acute land shortages, hunger and poor conditions. Rather, they would blame those who surrounded him at court. Government ministers (and by 1913 Rasputin) could therefore act as convenient scapegoats.

However, the image of the tsar as the protective father was severely damaged, at least from the perspective of the factory proletariat, by the Bloody Sunday massacre in 1905. It can be argued, too, that Nicholas forfeited the right to be seen as 'the father' when he took the fateful decision in 1915 to take personal command of the already catastrophic military campaigns on the eastern front. It would be increasingly difficult for even the peasantry to look upon Nicholas as father and protector amid the large-scale and increasingly pointless slaughter at the front.

A 'cult of personality'

It is not too much of an anachronism to suggest that a 'cult of personality' surrounded the tsar-autocrats. It was an essential and inevitable consequence of the autocratic political tradition. This cult of personality and the paternalistic aspect of Russian leadership were manifested even more dramatically under the Soviets. Lenin did not wilfully develop this cult — in fact, he actively resisted it. However, Stalin deliberately fostered the cult after Lenin's death, with the 'Lenin Enrolment' into the Communist Party, the renaming of Petrograd as Leningrad, the erection of huge statues of Lenin and the portrayal of Stalin himself as the great leader's natural heir, ally and successor. It was under Stalin that the paternalistic image and cult of personality reached extreme and absurd heights. School history textbooks were full of pictures of a larger-than-life 'Comrade Stalin' leading his peoples to a glorious socialist future. Not for nothing was Stalin often referred to as the 'Red tsar'. It is extraordinary that many of those millions of Russian peasants who suffered dreadfully during collectivisation continued to refer to Stalin as 'our little father'. They did not hold Comrade Stalin to blame for the excesses and tragedies of collectivisation, especially during the early years, but rather the corrupt party leaders and officials who deliberately misled the great leader and distorted his policies. It was this perception of the innate goodness of the great leader that enabled Stalin to get away with his notorious 'dizzy with success' speech in which he blamed 'certain party comrades' who had been overzealous in their harsh treatment of the peasantry in the early stages of collectivisation.

The power of ideology: the Russian Orthodox Church and the tsarist autocracy

Many of the examples given above suggest a profound, mystical bond between the tsar and his peoples. Another important reason for the institution of autocracy in Russia was the fact that the tsar ruled over a largely illiterate, politically immature population whose geographical horizons (and therefore, mental horizons) were limited severely. It is here that the political role of organised religion becomes important.

Of course, the empire comprised members of all the great religious faiths: Jews, for example, in the western parts, and Moslems in the more southern reaches. However, the official religion, and that practised by most of the 'Great Russians', was Russian Orthodoxy. Those who have witnessed a Russian Orthodox service will agree that in many respects this is a religion of the senses, sometimes described as 'pure theatre'. Such an institution has the potential for important power and political and social control over an undeveloped society. 'Mother Russia' was also 'Holy Russia'. The Church and its teachings underpinned the policy of 'Russification' of the empire towards the end of the nineteenth century. Insofar as Russian autocracy possessed an official ideology, it was that provided by Russian orthodoxy, whose nominal head was the tsar himself.

Russian orthodoxy provided the rationale, the *raison d'être* of the autocratic political system, and it embodied patriotism and Russian nationalism. To a large extent this helps to explain the popular image of the tsar as presented particularly to the peasantry. Clearly, the icons of the tsar referred to in 1913 and 1914 had strong religious and mystical connotations. The practical efficiency of the Church in Russia has recently been called into question, but that is another point. We are concerned here with the immense spiritual and propaganda value of the Church to autocracy. 'Holy Russia', 'peasant Russia', mysticism, political immaturity and the personal cult of the tsar-autocrat were in many senses all interlinked.

The most notorious example of the power of mysticism in the Russian autocracy is Rasputin. He was the quintessential Siberian 'peasant-monk'. The extraordinary religious sect which Rasputin is alleged to have joined in his youth was only one among hundreds that existed in nineteenth-century Russia. The reasons why an illiterate, dissolute and decadent figure could find himself at the centre of the Russian court (indeed, after 1915 effectively directing many military and political policies) are well known and well documented. His prominence was not due solely to the tsarevitch's haemophilia, which Rasputin could allegedly treat. As the representative of the 'real' peasant Russia, Rasputin was useful to Nicholas II. It is difficult to imagine any other major power in the world in the early twentieth century where such an extraordinary figure could come to be directing affairs at a time of total war.

The Bolsheviks, with their atheistic Marxist ideas, mounted an immediate and savage attack on the Russian Orthodox Church and its priests. However, not even Stalin in the 1930s was able to destroy it totally. Khrushchev also tried and failed in the 1950s. Perhaps the most telling point about the power of the Church is that the 'Red autocrat', the 'father of his peoples', Josef Stalin, actively reinvoked the power of the Church, encouraging attendance at church in Russia's hour of need during the Great Patriotic War after 1941. Thus Stalin followed the example of his autocratic predecessors by fusing patriotism, nationalism (surely an anti-Marxist concept) and religious ortho-doxy. To put it another way, if the Russian Orthodox Church could survive the most vicious onslaughts of a totalitarian regime in the 1930s, think how much power and influence it must have exerted when it provided the ideology and underpinning of the autocratic regimes before 1917.

The development of Soviet autocracy

Marxism-Leninism

It is tempting to state that, in effect, the ideology of Russian orthodoxy which under-pinned tsarist autocracy was replaced after 1917 by the ideology of Marxism-Leninism, which supported Soviet autocracy. Strictly speaking, this is incorrect. **Marxist** ideology implied collective forms of political organisation. The role of the party, refined by Engels, was to represent the collective will of the **proletariat**, not to place emphasis on any one leader. Indeed, after the phase of the 'dictatorship of the proletariat', according to Engels, the state (and by implication authoritarian rule by one leader) would 'wither away', a prediction repeated later by Lenin himself in his *State and Revolution*. This did not happen in Russia after 1917. On the contrary, the state (which came effectively to mean the Communist Party of the Soviet Union) exercised more power and control over the individual by the 1930s than it had ever done under the tsars, and the party itself had swollen in size. It was unrecognisable from the 'small tightly-knit group of dedicated professional revolutionaries' that Lenin had advocated earlier.

The great central question about the history of the Bolshevik revolution and development of the Soviet Union is how and why a revolution which claimed to be liberating the proletarian masses developed within little more than a decade into a political system which denied basic civil liberties and practised terror on a scale hitherto unknown in history. This had very little to do with Marxist ideology. There is nothing in Marx's writings to advocate the constant use of purges, forced labour camps, summary executions, forced collectivisation of agriculture, and liquidation of an entire class (the *kulaks*), all of which occurred under Stalin.

This is a huge question and space does not permit a detailed discussion here. The answer lies partly in the fact that, while Marx offered a profound and detailed critique of nineteenth-century bourgeois capitalist society, he was not specific on how the state and society should develop after the proletarian revolution. Even Lenin himself, in his many writings before October 1917, was more concerned with the revolutionary struggle than with the post-revolutionary exercise of power.

The fundamental explanation lies in the situation which Lenin and the Bolsheviks found themselves in after 1917. A small, urban-based party led by members of the intelligentsia had seized power in two cities (literally overnight in the case of Petrograd) in the name of, but with little real active support from, the proletariat. This happened in an empire totally unsuited to the conditions specified by Marx for a genuine proletarian revolution. Writing in the mid- to late-nineteenth century, Marx had reiterated that a society must go through its 'bourgeois-capitalist' phase before the proletarian one; thus the revolution should occur either in his native Germany or his adoptive Britain. In Marx's view, Russia was barely out of the feudal stage. This fact was appreciated fully by the Mensheviks, who were always the more literal inter- preters of Marx. This helps to explain their failure to oppose the Provisional Government in 1917, giving Trotsky the justification for consigning them to the 'dustbin of history' after the Bolshevik seizure of power.

Lenin was well aware that backward Russia was economically and socially unsuited to a genuine proletarian revolution. In his view this did not matter, because the task of the Russian Bolsheviks would be to take power in Russia and inspire their comrades in the more industrially advanced countries (particularly Germany) to follow suit. In this sense Lenin could claim not to be departing from Marxist ideology but following it, as the proletarian revolution would be genuinely international.

It should be borne in mind that events in 1917 took Lenin, and many others, by surprise. Famously, speaking in Zurich just before the fall of the tsar, he warned his audience that the revolution might have to wait for several decades. On his return to Russia in April he immediately grasped the reality of the situation, that 'power was waiting on the streets to be picked up'. By September, supported by the newly converted Trotsky, he had managed to convince the still sceptical Zinoviev, Kamenev, Bukharin and Stalin that conditions in war-torn Germany made a proletarian revolution there imminent and that 'history will not forgive us if we do not take power in Russia now'. Lenin's supreme opportunism only added to the difficulties in which the Russian Bolsheviks would soon find themselves.

These difficulties arose chiefly out of the fact that the expected revolution in Germany did not succeed and was never likely to occur in other advanced countries like Britain, France or the USA. Although there were lingering spartacist/socialist attempts in Berlin and Munich, any chance of a successful Bolshevik-style revolution in Germany had gone by 1920.

The significance of all this is that the Bolsheviks were forced into a bitter struggle simply to stay in power, and crucially that they became isolated in a potentially hostile world. The Cold War after 1945 effectively had its origins when the USA, France and Britain sent troops to help the Whites in their attempt to oust the Bolsheviks in 1919.

Stalinism

This is the essential background to the developments which led eventually to the Stalinist solution. The use of terror and the secret police (GPU, NKVD), the rigid suppression of trade unions and workers' control, the ruthless treatment of the peasantry by the grain requisition squads, the rigid imposition of censorship, and the effective denial of most civil liberties, were all justified as necessary. It was during the bitter struggle for power during the Civil War that the shape and future direction of the party and state were developed. The real roots of Stalinist autocracy can be found in this period, when the nature of the party and the conception of leadership changed fundamentally. Before the war, party leaders (chiefly intellectuals) had become used to free debate and internal elections. During the war, in the desperate struggle for survival in a hostile world, these were luxuries, as Lenin pointed out at the Tenth Party Congress in 1921. One of the most significant of all the party congresses, this adopted by a large majority decrees condemning any form of workers' opposition, and any deviation from the strict party line, which would be imposed increasingly from above.

Thus, within the space of 4 years, Russia had moved from an autocracy (which did allow the free existence of various political parties) to a multiparty republic, to a one-party state and, by 1921, a monolithic one-party state. However, it was not quite yet ruled in the autocratic fashion of the nineteenth-century tsars, who imposed personal leadership ruthlessly in a political system in which the masses had no say. It was Stalin's rise to power and, crucially, the imposition of 'socialism in one country' which were to complete the process. Suffering increasing illness, Lenin was effectively removed from the centre of power in 1922, although, of course, his authority was still unchallenged. It is tempting, but questionable, to say that the rise of Stalin to power from 1922 onwards was inevitable. By that date, he was General Secretary of the Party, was in control of the 'Workers' and Peasants' Inspectorate' and had been Commissar for Nationalities. It was the failure of Lenin's predicted revolutions in other, more advanced countries that made the 'Stalin solution' and the reimposition of an autocratic type of government the most likely outcome.

'Socialism in one country'

By imposing 'socialism in one country', Stalin was being pragmatic. The reality was that backward Russia needed to modernise rapidly on broadly socialist lines not just to catch up with the West but to defend the Soviet Union against an increasingly likely invasion. In fact, Stalin turned his back not just on the rest of the world but on Marxist-Leninist orthodoxy too. 'Socialism in one country' became enshrined in 'Marxism-Leninism-Stalinism', and it is here that Stalin's autocracy can be said to have been supported by Marxist ideology. Lenin had been constantly faithful to the assumption that the proletarian revolution would be an international phenomenon; so too had Trotsky. Stalinist ideology effectively turned Leninism on its head. Instead of the revolution in Russia inspiring revolutions in the more advanced countries so that they would aid and support the development of backward Russia, Russia would now develop on its own and, once fully developed, might then aid other countries to develop along socialist lines.

In order to achieve this extremely difficult task, total power had to be invested in one man, the leader. A cult of personality had to be imposed. The great leader had to be seen leading Russia to a glorious socialist future in the face of threats from a hostile world. A form of mystical faith was to surround the leader.

All this was almost unthinkable under Lenin. His dictatorship had used terror, but in the main, terror was used against those outside the party. Under Stalin, it was to be used against those within the party and state. Whereas under Lenin, some lip-service continued to be paid to internal party debates and policy discussions (at least until 1921), this was suppressed wholly under Stalin. It can be argued that Stalin's total power was not achieved fully until the murder of Kirov in 1934, sparking the major purges, but long before then Stalin was seen and referred to as 'the *vozhd*' (the boss).

Similarities between Stalin's rule and that of the tsars

With Stalin's accession to power, the Russian political tradition can be seen as reverting to its autocratic type in many respects. There were a number of similarities between Stalin's rule and that of the tsars: a personal form of government and a cult of personality; total power in the hands of one ruler; widespread use of the secret police; intolerance of any form of criticism or opposition; rigid censorship; a society ruled largely by fear; the banishment of political prisoners to the outer reaches of the empire; an autocratic form of government supported by an official ideology. As with the tsars, Stalin practised a 'Russification' of the empire, pursued an aggressively nationalist policy and inculcated fear and suspicion of the West; as with the tsars, there was widespread official anti-Semitism too.

The question of whether Stalin in some way deviated from, corrupted and distorted the system established by Lenin, or whether Stalinism was the logical and inevitable outcome of Leninism, is much debated. Some of the similarities and differences have been mentioned above. Much of the framework which underpinned Stalin's dictatorship had been developed by Lenin. However, the cult of personality was largely absent under Lenin. It was only after his death that Lenin was portrayed as an almost godlike figure. It is more likely that it was the *failure* of Lenin's expected revolutions elsewhere in the 1920s that created the Stalinist solution rather than Stalinism being the inevitable outcome of Leninism.

The similarities between tsarist and Stalinist autocracy should not be overestimated. Stalin's regime was far more brutal than that of any of the tsars. Stalin's Russia in the 1930s has often been held up as a classic example of the totalitarian state (far more so than Hitler's Germany). Totalitarianism, which as a political concept had its roots in the Roman Republic, was essentially and in practice a twentieth-century phenomenon. The practical ability and the technological capacity of the state to interfere in the lives of ordinary people, as it did under Stalin, did not exist before the industrial age. It is highly questionable whether the political aims of the tsars involved this form of intrusion and it is anachronistic to apply the word 'totalitarian' to any pre-twentieth century regime. 'Autocratic', 'authoritarian' and 'paternalistic' are more suitable words to use when pointing out the similarities between the forms of rule practised by the tsars and by Stalin.

Khrushchev's 'thaw'

Khrushchev has been credited with authorising a relaxation and dismantling of some of the more despotic and tyrannical aspects of Stalinism. In his famous 'De-Stalinisation' speech at the Twentieth Party Congress in February 1956, Khrushchev attacked Stalin's cult of personality and his abuses of power. Some of those purged during the 1930s were 'pardoned' and a number of *gulag* inmates were released. However, Khrushchev certainly did not intend to bring liberal reforms to the one-party system. His principal aim was to create a climate for his proposed economic reforms, and to aid his policy of 'peaceful co-existence' with the West during the Cold War. Although he was to be leader of the Soviet Union until his fall in 1964, his official title was First Secretary of the party. He ruled in a dictatorial fashion and his methods and the thinking behind them were just as autocratic as Stalin's, but there were far fewer victims and repression was less severe and on a smaller scale.

Glossary

Constituent Assembly: multiparty parliamentary assembly which had a very brief existence in January 1918 before being closed by the Bolsheviks
paternalistic: fatherlike
Marxist: following Karl Marx, the philosopher and economist who founded modern socialism and communism
proletariat: term used by Karl Marx to describe the industrial working class

Manifestations of autocracy

The development of the police state

From the **Okhrana** of the tsars to the KGB under Khrushchev, modern Russia has been characterised as a police state. This is an expression which is often overused. A police state can be defined as a political system in which there is a central political role for branches of the police and security services. These are often known as 'the secret police', and they are usually able to act independently from other government departments. Of course, the police can be said to have some form of political role in any political system, particularly when issues of national security are at stake. However, in liberal democracies and genuine multiparty, pluralist forms of government, it can be argued that there is no need for the police to have extra-ordinary powers of arrest and punishment, except in times of national emergency. 'Police states' or 'police dictatorships' are therefore associated more with dictatorial one-party systems in the twentieth century (Hitler's Gestapo, Stalin's NKVD) or authoritarian systems (the French Second Empire in the 1850s, Russia under Alexander III and Nicholas II).

Political police under the tsars

In Russia, the modern form of police state is said to have developed from the establishment by Nicholas I of the Third Section in 1826. Policing was split initially into three sections: the ordinary police, the gendarmerie and the Third Section, which dealt with informants and agents on political questions. The Third Section organised police surveillance, banishing suspicious persons and spying on and punishing those suspected of crimes against the state. Fundamentally, it dealt with state security and all political offences. It reported to the tsar directly; there was no opportunity to appeal against the system.

Punishment for political offences usually took the form of 'administrative exile' in Siberia, or imprisonment. Imprisonment, particularly in the notorious Peter and Paul Fortress, was often the harsher of the two punishments. It was usually members of the educated classes who were sent to Siberia. Exiles were forbidden to leave the destination to which they were sent, but could largely live within it how they pleased. This was far less draconian than the punishment regimes of the 1930s. It was during his Siberian exile in the 1890s that Lenin was able to formulate and write down many of his ideas on the organisation of the revolutionary party.

It can be said that the **codification** of Russian law under Nicholas I's minister Mikhail Speransky set the tone and mentality of the police state, as illustrated by this example from the 1845 code:

(1) All attempts to limit the authority of the sovereign or to alter the prevailing system of government, as well as persuade others to do so, or to give overt expression to such intentions, or to control, assist or fail to denounce anyone guilty of these offences, carry the death penalty and the confiscation of all property.

(2) The spreading by word of mouth or by means of the written or printed word of ideas which, without actually inciting to sedition, as defined above, raised doubts about the authority of the sovereign, or lessened respect for him or of his office, are punishable by the loss of civil rights and terms of hard labour from 4 to 12 years, as well as corporal punishment and branding.

Clearly, any form of public opposition to the autocracy could result in a sentence of hard labour, and any attempt to challenge it could result in death. If the word 'Stalin' were substituted for 'sovereign', this would not look out of place as a description of the powers of the NKVD in the 1930s. Obviously there are huge differences of scale, but the fundamental principles of the police state were laid. Under Nicholas I these harsh laws against political dissent were not easy to enforce, partly due to the poor communications in the empire, and also because the machinery of repression was still primitive. Between 1826 and 1861, fewer than 50,000 people were sent to Siberia. As late as 1901 there were an estimated 3,900 political exiles in Siberia, which is a low figure compared with the hundreds of thousands banished to the *gulag* under Stalin.

Thus tsarist Russia from the 1850s was effectively a police state, and as such it had a vested interest in the maintenance of fear and terror. Often, senior police officers could only rise to the highest posts by convincing the Minister of the Interior and the tsar that sedition and rebellion were permanently brewing beneath the surface. This mentality was the basis of the operation of the NKVD under Stalin. Under the tsars this could be used to justify lack of reform and political inertia, as all political reforms could be seen as dangerous.

The work of the Third Section increased in intensity during the 1870s because of the attempts on the tsar's life and the development of revolutionary terrorism. Its spying and invasions of privacy had led to notoriety and it was abolished in 1880, but its work was effectively continued by the Corps of Gendarmes, which operated directly under the Ministry of the Interior. By 1881 the membership of the Corps numbered 50,000. In that year a parallel secret police was established — the *Okhrana*. This had highly developed powers and more sophisticated forms of operation that were strengthened during the repressive rule of Alexander III. By this time the political police was acting overtly outside the normal agencies of the state, and its powers were virtually unrestricted. It could intercept mail, and operated by using spies and informers among ordinary workers and tradesmen, and by infiltrating 'subversive' organisations. By the 1890s and the early years of the twentieth century the *Okhrana* had spies in the factories and among the trade unions, and had infiltrated revolutionary movements like the Bolsheviks, the Mensheviks and the Socialist Revolutionaries. Because many of the leaders of these revolutionary parties were in exile abroad, it built up a sophisticated network of informants outside the empire.

Political police under Lenin

Immediately after the fall of Nicholas II, the Provisional Government abolished the hated *Okhrana*. Within 6 weeks of coming to power, the Bolsheviks established their own security police, the 'Extraordinary Commission for Struggle against Speculation and Counter-revolution,' or *Cheka*, under the Pole Felix Dzerzhinsky. This was initially to be a temporary organisation. Its immediate role was to root out agents of the enemy and counter-revolutionaries, and send them to the various revolutionary tribunals which had been established soon after the Bolshevik seizure of power.

The Bolsheviks were isolated, Russia was still nominally at war, and they had potential enemies ranging from the 'bourgeois' parties to tsarist army officers, including some elements among the peasantry and even members of the Menshevik and Socialist Revolutionary parties, not to mention looters, speculators, profiteers and German agents. It was almost inevitable in this situation that the *Cheka* should become a permanent organisation, and that its powers should grow. By the start of the Civil War in the summer of 1918, the *Cheka* employed around 40,000 agents. A number of these were ex-*Okhrana* officials. By this time, the revolutionary tribunals were being bypassed and summary executions were becoming commonplace — the chief victims were the former tsar and his family. After the attempted assassination of Lenin in September 1918, some 10,000 suspects were executed. During the Civil War the *Cheka* became the instrument of rule by terror.

With the end of the Civil War, there was some unease within the Bolshevik leadership about the indiscriminate use of terror by the *Cheka*, although it had been accepted as 'necessary' during the period of war communism. In 1922 the *Cheka* was abolished and replaced by the State Political Administration — the GPU. This was seen initially as an attempt to instil more discipline and end the summary executions. To a certain extent there was some relaxation of police terror during the NEP period. However, the political police continued the practices of the tsar's *Okhrana* by the imposition of internal exile in Siberia, or deportation abroad, for 'political undesirables'. In 1922 there was an ominous new development, the first show trial (of Socialist Revolutionary leaders)

Political police under Stalin

By the time Stalin had achieved supreme power in 1929, the apparatus of rule by terror by the political police was in place. Stalin's rule in the 1930s has become synonymous in the popular mind with the Reign of Terror, beginning with the purging and show trials of party leaders such as Zinoviev and Kamenev in 1936, the Red Army officers in 1937, and finally the purging of the secret police itself in 1938. It was under Stalin that the political police achieved the height of its power, especially from 1934. In that year the NKVD replaced the GPU, although nominally under the same leader, Yagoda.

Immediately after the assassination of Kirov in 1934, Stalin issued a decree which marked a return to the brutal methods and misuse of power of the Civil War. This laid down the procedure for dealing with all 'terrorist' organisations (i.e. all those for one reason or another suspected of being enemies of the state). The decree stated that investigations should not last for more than 10 days, cases were to be held in secret, there were to be no appeals, and death sentences were to be carried out immediately after sentencing. In order to find out who might be an enemy of the state, the NKVD created a wide network of informers who were told to report on aspects of behaviour, casual talk, jokes, social activities, morale, the general political mood and so on.

The Terror is widely assumed to have reached its height in 1937 and 1938. In the summer of 1937 Stalin, in conjunction with Yezhov (who had replaced Yagoda as head of the NKVD), drew up a specific list of those who were to be repressed and the punishments to be handed out. This was the notorious 'NKVD Order 00447'. Suspects were placed in two categories: those to be arrested immediately and shot (after brief 'investigation') and those 'less hostile elements' who were to be sent to a labour camp for 8–10 years. Those listed as 'groups to be repressed' were former *kulaks*, members of anti-Soviet parties (Socialist Revolutionaries, Georgian Mensheviks and members of opposition groups within the nationalities), former Whites, tsarist policemen and civil servants, bandits, dealers and returnees from emigration, White Cossacks, 'fascist-terrorist and espionage-diversionary counter-revolutionary groups', 'churchmen', cattle and horse thieves and criminal elements in camps and work colonies.

This, then, was a very long list of potential suspects; it was all-embracing, and gave widespread licence to the local members of the NKVD. What is most significant is that attached to this list was a list of numbers (not names) of those to be 'repressed', broken down into categories 1 and 2. This comprised 'suspects' in 64 regions of the USSR and numbered well over 100,000. A sum of 75 million roubles was granted to the NKVD for the purpose. In the event, these targets, which had been drawn up by Yezhov, were by a long way exceeded and Stalin himself authorised an extra 48,000 executions at the beginning of 1938. This is a classic illustration of the powers of the political police under Stalin. It was the responsibility of the relevant local NKVD boss to meet, or even exceed, Yezhov's targets in which ever way he chose, just as it was the responsibility of the local factory manager to meet the quotas in the Five Year Plans. The wide category of potential suspects (effectively anybody who could be classified as 'anti-Soviet') and the initiative given from above to local NKVD bosses have led some historians to assert that it was effectively the political police rather than Stalin himself who ruled the Soviet Union.

The worst ravages of the Great Terror were over by the end of 1938. Yezhov was demoted and then 'disappeared', to be replaced by Beria. The Great Patriotic War required close surveillance of the population, and the duties of the political police extended to espionage. After 1945 a new category of potential 'suspects' was added: those unfortunate soldiers in the Red Army who had been captured and put into Nazi concentration camps. These were now suspect because they had become 'tainted' with Nazi ideology, and tens of thousands of liberated Red Army officers now found themselves in the *gulag* — perhaps the most famous was the writer Alexander Solzhenitsyn. There was no significant relaxation of the powers of the NKVD; indeed a new purge, possibly to exceed the scale of those of 1937–38, was being planned by Beria at the time of Stalin's death in 1953.

Political police under Khrushchev

The powers and activities of the NKVD had caused such fear, particularly among party leaders, that it is not surprising that the political police was brought under tighter control under Khrushchev. Beria was executed within months of Stalin's death, and the NKVD was abolished. The whole secret police system was reorganised, many NKVD leaders were dismissed and a Committee of State Security was established — the KGB. The atrocities committed by the NKVD were denounced by Khrushchev in his 'De-Stalinisation' speech in 1956, and not surprisingly the focus of the new political police, at the height of the Cold War, shifted somewhat from the 'enemy within' to espionage, although the basic political police functions of the KGB remained similar to those of its predecessors.

From the *Okhrana* to the KGB

The scale, role and extraordinary powers of the political police under the Bolsheviks far exceeded anything under the tsars. The reasons are obvious and most of them have been discussed above. However, it is the *tradition* of the police state which should be emphasised. In this respect, just as the tsarist autocrats ruled to an extent by fear, so too did the Bolsheviks. The mentality of the average *Okhrana* official in, say, 1900 would not be unlike that of his NKVD counterpart in 1937. Both would rely on rumours, gossip and local denunciations, and both would have a vested interest in casting suspicion on potential enemies and colleagues alike. It was a system which bred sycophancy. A possible difference is that the activities of the *Okhrana* were easier to keep in check than those of the NKVD. It is not surprising, as mentioned above, that many members of the newly formed *Cheka* in 1918 came from the ranks of the former *Okhrana*.

> **Glossary**
>
> ***Okhrana***: secret police force established in **1881**
> **codification**: classification and centralisation of Russian laws

The top-down nature of reforms and initiatives

A tendency in autocratic systems of government which can be dealt with quite briefly here is for initiatives to come from above. This is hardly surprising in a political system which under both the tsars and the Bolsheviks lacked any independent representative or civic institutions. A lack of genuine consultation from below can help to explain the flawed, sometimes rushed, nature of the implementation of policies.

Under the tsars

Alexander II's emancipation of the serfs was not rushed through — it took 5 years from his statement that it was 'better to emancipate the serfs from above rather than wait until they abolish serfdom from below' to the publication of the Emancipation Edict. Nonetheless, while the government entered into discussions with the nobility about ways and means, it did not consult the serfs themselves. Essentially, the terms and conditions were decided on by the State Council, the leaders of the Moscow nobility and the tsar. The village *mir*, which was to be so important in the implementation of the edict, was not consulted. When the terms of emancipation were announced to the peasantry (often by the local priest) there could be no discussion and in many cases there were detachments of police present to prevent any disturbances provoked by disappointment.

In the same spirit of 'rule and reform from above', the fundamental task of the notorious land captains (mainly recruited from among the gentry), introduced in 1889, was to restrict the local influences of the various *mir* and village assemblies, in other words to stifle local initiatives in an attempt to retain total political control. It was during the reign of Alexander III that any local initiatives given by Alexander II's reforms were curtailed. For example, any self-government initiated by the *zemstva* was restricted by tightening the qualifications for elections to the assemblies, to give more weight to the higher reaches of the middle classes and the landowners.

Witte's 'Great Spurt' was essentially hurried through from above. The state played a key role in investment and loans to industry, as consumer of industrial products and importer of foreign loans and capital. One important political consequence of this, as has been seen, was that it inhibited the development of a strong and independent middle class. The industrial and business classes which flourished during the rapid industrialisation were still largely dependent on the state.

In a sense, this notion of initiatives coming from above can also be applied to the circumstances of the fall of Nicholas II in 1917 and the establishment of the Provisional Government. While the bread queues, strikes, riots and demonstrations on the streets of Petrograd in February 1917 were clearly a crucial element in the fall of the tsar, it should not be forgotten that the key element in his abdication was the decision taken from above by Duma and military leaders that the tsar must go. It was the desertion of Nicholas by the military elite which caused him finally to see the writing on the wall. Traditionally, the fall of Nicholas has been portrayed as a spontaneous revolution from below, but in a real sense this was a 'revolution from above'. Similarly, the Provisional Government took power from above without any mandate from below. The 'legitimisation' of the new government by the election of a Constituent Assembly was put off until after the war.

Under the Bolsheviks

The same point can be made about the Bolshevik seizure of power in October. In reality this was a coup from above by the comparatively small Bolshevik Military Revolutionary Committee. Despite retrospective attempts to portray the seizure as some kind of large-scale workers' uprising and storming of the Winter Palace, the reality was that the revolution was imposed on the Russian people from above.

The introduction of the NEP in 1921 is a similar case. To all intents and purposes this was Lenin's own policy. There was widespread reluctance to adopt this policy among the *Politburo* and Central Committee of the party. The NEP was introduced by Lenin at the Tenth Party Congress in 1921. The policy was essentially steamrollered through by Lenin, after he had threatened to resign. There was no genuine debate or discussion.

Under Stalin and Khrushchev

Perhaps the best example of reforms and initiatives being forced through from above is the introduction of the Five Year Plans and collectivisation of agriculture by Stalin. The 'Stalin revolution' of the 1930s has often been referred to as a 'revolution from above' with good reason. Between 27 December 1929 (the date of Stalin's notorious 'liquidate the *kulaks*' speech) and the autumn of 1930, collectivisation was to be carried out among all farms in the big grain-producing areas, and total collectivisation of all agriculture was to be completed by 1932. The idea of collectivisation had been discussed by the party leadership after the grain procurements crisis of 1927, and once Bukharin had been removed from the *Politburo* in 1929 the way was clear for Stalin to institute collectivisation. The whole programme was officially described in propaganda as 'voluntary' on the part of the peasants. In reality, only the minority of poor peasants were willing to comply. Collectivisation was rushed through and forced on the peasantry from above, and this partly explains the disasters in Russian agriculture in the 1930s.

The Five Year Plans for industry operated from the top downwards, too. *Gosplan*, the State Planning Commission, set overall targets for each industry. Each region was given targets, and mines and factories within each region were given targets in turn. Within each local enterprise, managers set targets for each foreman, and individual workers were given targets for each shift. This hierarchical structure took little account of local conditions. Of course, foremen and workers on the factory floor devised their own ways and means of meeting the targets, and in this sense there was room for local initiative, but the point is that the target was set from above and had to be met. Managers, foremen and workers were told what to produce and how much.

Khrushchev did make attempts to allow some decentralisation and more local initiatives in both industry and agriculture, but he did not depart from the tradition of rushing through 'reforms' from above. For example, his Virgin Lands Campaign and the scheme for wholesale cultivation of maize took little account of local conditions, and allowed little room for local initiative.

The weakness of opposition

An obvious reason for the maintenance and survival of autocratic forms of government was the weakness of opposition. Of course, opposition existed to both the tsars and the Bolsheviks. In particular, this developed in the 1860s as a consequence of Alexander II's reforms, and continued under the Bolsheviks, even under Stalin. However, opposition to autocracy can be seen to have failed.

It should be remembered that it was not organised opposition which brought down the tsarist autocracy in 1917. To a very large extent, Nicholas II fell; he was not really pushed by opponents. He fell because his military and political elite (the 'reluctant revolutionaries') deserted him in February 1917. They were forced to make the choice between 'mother Russia's' survival in the war and loyalty to the tsar.

Similarly, there was opposition to Bolshevik rule not just from outside the party, but also from within it. The Kronstadt Rebellion of 1921 revealed the extent of disillusionment within the party. There was a great deal of controversy and opposition to the NEP and Stalin's methods in the 1930s; collectivisation, particularly, aroused opposition and criticism. Again, this came to nothing and was crushed.

Under both the tsars and the Bolsheviks, opposition came essentially from the 'intelligentsia' — a term of Russian origin. In the nineteenth century the intelligentsia, broadly speaking, comprised all those who had had some form of meaningful education. The term came to have a rather looser definition than in the West. Inevitably, given the sociological development of Russia at the time, the intelligentsia came originally from the nobility, the only class until the 1860s which had any real form of education. After Alexander II's broadening of educational opportunities in the 1860s, the social background of the intelligentsia changed somewhat. Although many were still nobles, or of noble origin, increasingly members of what might be termed the middle classes joined their ranks. There was thus a marked change both in the quantity and quality of the intelligentsia between the essentially aristocratic, smaller and more subservient generation of the 1840s (the 'fathers' in Turgenev's novel *Fathers and Sons*) and the increasingly more radical and, in extreme cases, nihilistic generation of the 1860s (the 'sons'). It was the members of a more socially diluted intelligentsia (the *raznochintsy*) who formed the basis of opposition to tsarist rule. During the later decades of the nineteenth century, opposition to tsarist rule came from three broad areas: liberalism, Marxism and populism. The first two were of Western inspiration; populism was essentially in the Russian tradition.

The failure of Russian liberalism

Until 1906 there was no legal form of opposition to tsarist autocracy, and therein lay a major problem for Russian liberals. They had no clearly defined forum in which to oppose the tsar and his policies. The coming of the *zemstva* and municipal councils as part of Alexander II's local government reforms did offer some small beginnings and a valuable training ground for the political liberal opposition after 1906, but they were socially isolated and operated in a vacuum.

Another problem was that Russian liberals were viewed with great suspicion by the autocracy. They advocated many of the same things as their western European counterparts in the nineteenth century: freedom of speech and worship, basic civil liberties, equality before the law, a constitution and a nationally elected parliament. All these ideas ran counter to tsarist ideology, and there was no room for compromise. The autocracy could not tolerate criticism or opposition of any kind. Alexander III and Nicholas II made no real distinction between liberalism and the infinitely more dangerous revolutionary socialism. Criticism was criticism, and should be suppressed wherever it came from. This was a major mistake. The net result was to turn what might have been relatively harmless and moderate critics of the tsars into implacable opponents.

Russian liberalism developed gradually in the later nineteenth century. Its natural breeding ground was among students and academics at the universities, and it took an active role in the events of the Revolution of 1905. After 1906, the *Kadets* were the main liberal party in the Dumas and the mainstay of the Provisional Government in 1917.

However, liberal opposition failed drastically, as has already been seen. Not only were Russian liberals isolated sociologically and by definition a strict minority, they were also isolated geographically. Their places of influence were the universities and the professions in the major cities. The vast mental, sociological and geographical gulf between them and the nobility, the industrial workers in the factories and, of course, the vast hordes of semi-literate peasants, was to be crucial. Moreover, Russian liberals can be accused of only wanting the kinds of freedom that were of interest to them: freedom in the university curriculum, autonomy for universities, a voting franchise extending only to the middle classes, and so on. In other words, the liberals concentrated overwhelmingly on narrow political issues rather than more pressing social and economic ones.

The failure of Russian populism

Populism in the nineteenth century was a Russian phenomenon. Russian populist agitators were members of the intelligentsia who advocated a peculiarly Russian form of socialism. In their view, Russia should bypass the capitalist stages of Western economic development, and make the Russian peasant the focal point of a socialist utopia. The basis would not be the factory floor or some nationally elected parliament, but the traditional village commune — the *mir*. The populists saw the commune as a 'natural' socialist form of organisation, with its supposed emphasis on egalitarianism in land holdings. Agrarian socialism, and the key to Russia's future, lay in Russia turning its back on Western forms of development. This line of thinking found its greatest expression in the work of Chernyshevsky, whose book, *What is to be done?* (1862), insisted that a social revolution was far more important than a political one.

Russian peasants should be guided towards socialism by encouragement; it should not be forced on them from above. The peasants and the village commune were 'natural' socialists and it should be the task of the intelligentsia to 'go to the people' and show them the way.

The trouble was that Russian peasants were not interested in being 'shown the way'. Between 1874 and 1876 hundreds of revolutionary activists, mainly students of middle- and upper-class origin, went out into the villages to try to persuade the peasants of their socialist instincts. And they failed almost totally. Village peasants saw them as an alien group, as outsiders interfering in their own parochial existence. Many were simply chased out of the villages, and many more were denounced to the local author- ities; some were even killed. Despite populist rhetoric about not imposing socialism from above, that was essentially what they were trying to do. The abject failure of 'going to the people' is a classic illustration of the vast gulf between the elites and the uneducated masses, which characterised so much of Russian politics and society in the nineteenth century. It is also a further illustration of the innate traditionalism and conservatism of the Russian peasantry.

This failure led to more radical initiatives. In 1876 a movement known as 'Land and Liberty' was formed in recognition that more direction should be given in leading the peasants to socialism. This was a secret organisation and highly disciplined. It advocated the use of terrorism and assassinations of leading figures within the ruling elite. Its most prominent assassination attempt was on the life of the governor of St Petersburg in 1878, which led to the famous trial and acquittal of Vera Zasulich.

'Land and Liberty' was superseded by the terrorist organisation, the 'People's Will', in 1878–79. In its view, social revolution would be sparked by shock tactics. Its most famous victim was the tsar himself, Alexander II, who was killed in March 1881. This spectacular 'success' was in fact a failure for the movement. It alarmed many liberals and more moderate opponents of the tsar, and therefore lost potential support. It also brought to the throne Alexander III, who almost immediately instigated a ruthless clampdown on terrorist activity, forcing populist leaders into exile abroad.

The 'failure' of Russian Marxism

It might seem odd to describe Russian Marxism as a failure before 1917, but it was only after the fall of the tsars that Marxism succeeded. During the 1870s, tracts of translated Marxist literature were being smuggled into Russia and circulated among students. Most of those who became the original leading advocates of Marxism, people like Plekhanov, were in exile in western Europe.

Marxism shifted the focal point from the peasantry to the urban proletariat. The problem was that the conditions for a Marxist-style revolution did not exist at this time in Russia. Marx had stipulated that society must go through stages: from the feudal to the bourgeois-capitalist phase. It was only after a society had had its 'bourgeois revolution' that work could begin on the 'proletarian revolution'.

The way such potential opposition was dealt with was shown as early as 1928, with the trial of 53 mining engineers from the Donbass region. This was the 'Shakhty trial', in which the accused were supposed to have plotted to sabotage the economy. It was claimed that they were in the pay of former White agents and foreign conspirators. In the event, only five of the 'guilty' were executed, but the Shakhty trial opened the way for the fundamental charges which would be brought against the accused in the show trials of the 1930s — that not only were they plotting against the state and Stalin (usually in the pay of the exiled Trotsky), but that by sabotaging the great achievements of the Five Year Plans they were guilty of unpatriotic measures against the state, 'socialist' or otherwise.

In the circumstances of the 1930s, the show trials were a powerful weapon. To oppose Stalin and his policies was to oppose the party. To oppose the party was to oppose the state, and to oppose the state was to be in the pay of fascist organisations in the West. The party was in effect the state, and thanks largely to the earlier work of Lenin, Bolsheviks had been educated to believe in 'my party, right or wrong'. The accusation of crimes against the party was the killer blow for the victims of the show trials, and nearly all of them pleaded guilty.

The Great Terror and the imposition of a ruthless form of totalitarianism, rule by the secret political police and an atmosphere of fear and suspicion obviously explain the lack of effective opposition to Stalin's policies. After the Terror there continued to be some limited opposition, but this was on a small scale, isolated and scattered.

The weakness of opposition to Khrushchev

Under the 'Khrushchev thaw' after the death of Stalin, there were increased opportunities for potential opponents to voice their opinions. There was widespread shock and criticism after the revelations in the 'De-Stalinisation' speech, and there were growing criticisms of some of Khrushchev's policies. However, in some ways, despite his more liberal approach, Khrushchev had major advantages over his opponents. As First Secretary he had control over the party machine and this enabled him to overcome opposition from the 'anti-party group'. Moreover, during the height of the Cold War in the 1950s, patriotism was given renewed force. By this time the CPSU numbered several millions (instead of having 'withered away') and opposition to it was as futile as under Stalin. Khrushchev's own position seemed secure until the Cuban missile crisis of 1962 and the failed harvests of the 1960s.

Glossary

libertarian: freedom-conscious individual

Exploitation of the peasantry and industrial working classes

Exploitation of the peasantry

The peasantry in modern Russia tended to be treated by the tsars and the Bolsheviks as an exploitable underclass. Both under the tsars and after 1917, the Russian peasant was often referred to as a *muzhik*, which is a somewhat affectionate although rather patronising term. The *muzhik* was seen by the tsarist autocracy as the very embodiment of Holy Russia and during the 1920s as a vital part of the **smychka**, the link with the proletarian masses. However, in reality the ruling elites within the tsarist bureaucracy and the Bolshevik party never understood the peasantry — not surprisingly, since they rarely had any contact with them. Under the tsars and the Bolsheviks, there remained a vast economic, cultural and social gap between the urban elites and the rural poor. There were indeed 'two Russias'.

In private, Stalin liked to identify with and indulge in Georgian peasant traditions and customs. Khrushchev, born into a poor peasant family, never failed to emphasise his peasant roots and his self-proclaimed expertise in agricultural matters. However, in modern Russia the peasant has been the *object* of history, exploited and exploitable, always the poorest and least privileged group or class in Russian society.

Until 1861, the majority of peasants suffered under serfdom. There were 50 million state- or privately-owned serfs. Serfs farmed land allotted to them, and in return were required to work for 3–4 days per week on the landlord's land. The serf owner could increase or decrease the amount of time to be spent on his own land at will. He could seize a serf's property, force them to become domestic servants, force or forbid them to marry, prevent a serf from leaving the village, and sell a serf and his family for profit to another landowner. The landowner had legal jurisdiction over his serfs except in cases of murder, and could authorise or administer punishments such as whipping, exile to Siberia or sending a serf into the army. Should the tsar require it, a serf could be conscripted into the army for up to 25 years' military service.

This brutal system, which had been abandoned in western Europe long before, formed the basis of the Russian economic, military, legal and local government systems under Nicholas I's autocracy. Nicholas had considered abolishing it, but was faced with the powerful vested interests of the nobility, and had simply tinkered at the edges by relaxing some of the harsher measures.

However, towards the end of his reign, some of the more enlightened senior government officials were urging abolition on humanitarian grounds. The more enterprising landowners had come to realise that free wage labour was more appropriate for the development of large-scale industry and business. Even before the Crimean War there were signs that the serfs themselves were demanding abolition, using violent measures. In the 10 years before the accession of Alexander II there were 400 outbreaks of peasant disturbances, with a further 400 between 1855 and 1861. Nearly 300 landowners and bailiffs were killed during this period. It was this that prompted Alexander II's famous speech of 1856, stating that it was better to abolish serfdom from above than to wait until the serfs abolished it themselves.

This was the background to the Emancipation Edict of 1861, but its immediate cause was the humiliating defeat of the serf-based Russian army in the Crimean War. It took the new tsar, in conjunction with the nobles, nearly 5 years to work out the ways and means of emancipation. When news and rumours of the intended emancipation filtered down to the villages, Alexander was hailed as the 'tsar-liberator'.

Continued exploitation after emancipation

Finally, in March 1861, the emancipation decree was issued. The Russian peasants were now technically free subjects. They could marry whoever they wanted (even women could choose their husbands), they could own property, set up businesses and engage in legal action if they could afford to.

However, it was not long before the ways in which emancipation was carried out, and its precise terms, caused bitter disappointment. The traditional village commune (the *mir*) was charged with overseeing and administering emancipation. Its powers were strengthened and in many ways it assumed the powers of the former landlords. It collected taxes, was responsible for maintaining order locally, selected recruits for the military, and supervised land allocations and distribution. Importantly, the *mir* had to agree if a peasant wanted to move away from the village. This was significant as one of the main aims of emancipation was to facilitate the mobility of labour for industry.

It seemed that the peasants had exchanged one master (the landlord) for another (the *mir*). In practice, the extent of the legal freedoms of the peasants was limited; they still had special courts and were yet to be given full citizens' rights — they had fewer rights under the law than their social superiors. This lack of genuine political freedom was accentuated by the imposition of the land captains after 1889. Theoretically, their role was to oversee the rights of the peasantry. They were given widespread powers of imposing fines and prison terms. Often, however, these powers were abused and many land captains simply oppressed the peasants even further.

It was in the area of economic freedom that the peasantry suffered the most. The restrictions imposed by the *mir* on crop selection, rotation of land, the massive burden of redemption payments, and the reduction in the amount of land available to the peasants, coupled with a dramatic rise in the rural population, left the bulk of the Russian peasantry impoverished. It was the unexpected imposition of redemption payments which caused most concern. In the first 4 months after emancipation, there were 647 peasant riots and disturbances in western Russia. In the province of Kazan, 100 peasant rioters were killed by troops. The peasants demanded a 'second emancipation', but in response the tsar said in 1861: 'There will be no emancipation except the one I have given you. Obey the laws and statutes! Work and toil! Obey the authorities and the landowners.'

By the late 1870s, many peasants were in arrears over their redemption payments. By 1880 there was an average shortfall of over 20% in the amount of money paid to the state. In northern Russia the figure was 46%. The state therefore reduced the overall amount owed by 25%. Peasants lost their right to graze animals and gather firewood on the common lands in the villages. There were regional variations, but on average peasants received 25% less land to own than they had farmed as serfs. Moreover, they still did not technically own the land. Title deeds to land were retained by the *mir* until all redemption payments had been paid.

From the 1880s onwards the most serious problem facing peasant households was shortage of land, made worse by the rapid population growth. The average size of allotments of land belonging to peasants fell from 35 acres in 1887 to 28 acres by 1905. The productivity of the land was reduced gradually as land was constantly re-worked and re-used without adequate fertilisation. This was not helped by the impact of the various agricultural crises in Europe in the late 1880s. The almost inevitable consequence of all this was a great famine in 1891–92. It is estimated that nearly half a million rural inhabitants died as a result. Large-scale, devastating famines were to be a feature of rural Russian life right up until 1949.

Exploitation under Witte in the 1890s

Witte can be accused of under-investing in agriculture as part of his 'Great Spurt', but it is perhaps unfair to blame him for causing peasant poverty and misery. It is more correct to say that he, like his predecessors and successors, continued to treat the peasants as exploitable objects. As with the Bolsheviks in the late 1920s and Stalin in the 1930s, the aim was to squeeze the peasants in order to pay for rapid industrialisation. One of the measures was to impose indirect taxes on commodities like vodka, tobacco and fuel. The logic was that high taxation would force peasants to sell grain which could be used for export. Russian peasants were seen simply as a source of revenue. Given the widespread general poverty of most peasants (for example, 30% of peasant farmers did not possess even a single horse), it is not surprising that periodic food shortages and famines were almost a built-in feature of peasant life. There was a growing wave of peasant riots and disturbances in 1902–03 and again during the revolution of 1905–06.

The misery of all this has been brilliantly evoked by Orlando Figes in *A People's Tragedy* (Vintage/Ebury, 1997). He paints vivid pictures of the savagery and innate conservatism and traditionalism of rural life at the turn of the century. This was a world of violence, crime and drunkenness. There were exceptions, and indeed some peasants did become prosperous *kulaks*, almost 'gentry' farmers, but the difficulty in raising capital, the 'protective' security provided by the *mir*, and the general lack of an entre-preneurial spirit were serious impediments.

Stolypin's 'new' approach after 1907

Stolypin's agricultural reforms mark a shift in attitude and emphasis in peasant affairs. As prime minister he was undoubtedly the first senior government official to view the peasantry as something more than simply an exploitable class. However, Stolypin was operating in isolation. Within ruling circles he was feared and distrusted, both by the reactionaries and the progressives, who saw him as the tsar's 'hatchet man' in the repressive atmosphere of the post-revolutionary period of 1906–07, and he was assassinated in 1911.

The abolition of the hated redemption payments had already been promised by the tsar at the end of 1905. Stolypin aimed to reduce the power of the *mir* over the local peasantry; to allow peasants to have complete freedom in leaving their village if they wished; to give greater encouragement and incentives to private enterprise in farming by encouraging peasants to consolidate isolated strips of land into one, larger farm; and to reduce the repressive powers of the land captains. Peasants were given financial assistance to buy land. It was hoped that a strong *kulak* class of peasants would emerge in sufficient numbers to provide solid social and political support for autocracy, and to form the large-scale consumer market required for industry.

The success or failure of Stolypin's reforms has been subject to historical debate and controversy. The reforms were not given the 20 years that Stolypin required, being interrupted by the outbreak of war in 1914. It is estimated that between 1906 and 1916 some 20% of the peasantry had left the *mir*. The trend towards consolidation of land strips was declining by 1914 and it seems that the majority of Russian peasants preferred the security of the traditional village commune and feared breaking out into the unknown. It is true that there was a decline in peasant riots from 3,000 in 1905–06 to 130 in 1914, but there is some evidence that the deliberate attempt to create a *kulak* class caused bitterness and resentment in many villages, something which the Bolsheviks were to capitalise on in the later 1920s. Stolypin's reforms in the end did little to remove the misery of the Russian peasant's lot. By 1917 there was still a great 'land hunger' and poverty was rife in rural Russia.

Exploitation under the Bolsheviks

The great majority of the millions of Russian soldiers, poorly led and badly equipped, who suffered on the eastern front were peasants in uniform. Just as they had been treated as fodder for Witte's industrialisation policies, now they were treated as fodder for German and Austrian cannons. After the fall of Nicholas II, peasants appeared to be given new hope by the exhortations of the Bolsheviks to 'go home and seize the land', but with the outbreak of civil war in 1918 they were soon to be disillusioned. The Russian peasantry suffered greatly under the policies of war communism.

Under the tsars, at least some lip-service had been paid to the notion of the *muzhik* as the 'bedrock' and 'soul' of 'mother Russia'. Now, under the Bolsheviks, they were to be deprived even of that. This was partly a reflection of Marxist doctrine. It was to be the industrial proletariat who would replace the peasantry as the 'bedrock' of the new society. Moreover, the majority of Bolshevik leaders did not come from the peasantry and in reality had little genuine interest in, or knowledge of, peasant mentalities, desires, or customs. It is hardly surprising that the new regime should continue to treat the peasantry as an exploitable underclass.

Under war communism, Trotsky in particular aimed for the 'militarisation' of industry and agriculture. The problem was the food supply. The small-scale, backward Russian agriculture would have to provide food for the Red Army and the urban population. There was a lack of consumer goods or money to trade with the peasants, so the Bolsheviks used force in what was unfortunately termed the 'battle for grain'. The Bolsheviks' lack of understanding of the peasant mentality was also revealed in their decree on 'Socialist Land Organisation' of 1919, which saw the beginnings of the collective farm system. Not only was collectivised, socialist farming totally alien to the petty capitalist mentality and traditions of the peasantry, but these experimental collectives were run by party officials who knew very little about farming matters. However, what the peasants came to hate and fear the most were the notorious 'grain requisition squads'. Grain hoarders were often shot by firing squads, and not surprisingly peasants tended to retreat into subsistence farming, contributing to the disastrous famine of 1921–22.

It wasn't just the Reds who treated the peasants badly. Peasant villages were looted and destroyed by the Whites too. Many of those who actively supported the Reds did so because they saw them as the lesser of two evils.

The situation of the peasants under the NEP

It is tempting to regard the period of the NEP and the abandonment of war communism as a period of relaxation of the exploitation of the peasantry. This is not strictly true. Although the incentive to grow food surpluses was provided by the private market and attempts were made to incorporate the peasantry into the new socialist order by emphasising the 'link' (*smychka*) between the peasant and the worker, in reality the party leadership increasingly manipulated the system to squeeze more grain from the peasants. In practice, this meant constantly raising the grain quota figures — the quantities of grain the peasants had to supply to the state before selling any surplus on the private market. This was much disputed and debated in party leadership circles before Stalin rendered the whole system irrelevant in the 1930s.

The Bolsheviks also betrayed their lack of understanding of the peasants by classifying them into 'poor', 'middle' and '*kulak*' peasants. In fact, many of those unfortunates who fell into the *kulak* category would in the West have been labelled as 'poor' peasants. Grotesque images of the fat, greedy and grasping *kulaks* were produced by party leaders even before Stalin announced his intention to 'liquidate them as a class'.

Exploitation under Stalin

It was under Stalin that the peasantry suffered as never before. The scale and intensity of the exploitation of the peasantry under Stalin mark him out from his predecessors, rather than the principle of exploitation. As under Witte, the peasants, forcibly herded into giant collective farms, were essentially to pay the costs of rapid industrialisation. To facilitate this, class warfare was encouraged in the countryside. The denunciation of *kulaks* was encouraged and their property was confiscated and handed over to the collective. Many of the victims were by no stretch of the imagination prosperous. Some *kulaks*, having destroyed or consumed their livestock and produce rather than turn it over to the collective, fled the villages, hoping to avoid the authorities and gain work in the factories. Some were allowed land in the neighbourhood not required by the collective. This, by definition, would be the very poorest land. The majority were sent into exile to remote regions in Siberia. Many of those who showed active signs of resistance were simply shot. Figures vary, but it has been estimated that up to 7 million *kulaks* suffered in this way.

The ravages of collectivisation coupled with poor weather and a poor grain harvest in 1931 led to the great famine of 1932. Again, figures vary, but at the most pessimistic level it has been estimated that 10 million rural inhabitants died. The famine occurred during the first Five Year Plan when Stalin desperately needed vast quantities of grain for export. The famine was therefore kept a secret from the urban population and foreign journalists. International relief organisations were not involved, since Stalin feared that foreign countries might cease importing Soviet grain during the crisis.

Life in the collective farms was, by Western standards, grim. The Russian peasants were reduced even further in status. They lacked sufficient income, were unable to purchase consumer goods, and were subject to rigid political control, usually by the Machine Tractor Stations in each locality. They were subject to domination by collective farm chairmen who were often party *apparatchiks* with little knowledge about farming matters. Despite the fact that under the Kolkhoz Charter of 1935 peasants had the right to keep a few domestic animals, cultivate small private plots and sell some produce on the black market, this in no way compensated them adequately. It was the Russian industrial worker who was the 'hero of Soviet labour'. It was the industrial proletariat who were hailed as the builders of the 'great socialist future', not the exploitable and exploited peasantry who remained essentially second-class citizens in the 'workers' state'.

As during the First World War, the peasantry suffered disproportionately during the Great Patriotic War after 1941. The overwhelming majority of the estimated 27 million Soviet citizens who perished in that conflict came from the peasantry. Those in the western parts of the Soviet Union suffered under occupation by the Nazis, too. The fact that many Ukrainian peasants welcomed the Nazi invaders initially speaks volumes for their sufferings under Stalin. These unfortunate people became victims of Nazi ideology and were treated not so much as an exploitable underclass, but as members of an inferior, subhuman race.

During the remaining years of Stalin's rule, the lives of the peasants did not improve significantly. The peasants who hoped that collectivisation would be abandoned as a reward for victory in war were soon disillusioned. A decree of 1946 authorised increases of grain quotas to be supplied to the state at reduced prices, impoverishing the peasants still further. Rather than abandon collective farming, Stalin aimed for a more ruthless implementation of it. The poverty of socialist farming was made even worse by the drastic gender imbalance in the population after the war, as so many male peasants had been killed during the war. In 1946 came another drought and resulting famine, in which an estimated 1 million rural inhabitants died. During the period 1945–53, therefore, the peasants were even more underprivileged and poverty-stricken.

Khrushchev's initiatives

Khrushchev was proud of his peasant origins and made genuine attempts to improve Russian agriculture and the lives of peasants. Incentives were meant to replace Stalinist coercion and exploitation. However, while it is true that peasants had more opportunities to purchase consumer goods, and attempts were made to modify the worst features of collectivised agriculture, Khrushchev did not abandon the collective farm system, which was the basis of the misery of millions of peasants.

Conclusions

Throughout the period from the accession of Alexander II to the arrival of Khrushchev in power, the peasants were exploited, manipulated, kept in dire poverty, misunderstood by the ruling classes (whether tsarist or Soviet), and generally treated as objects.

One might argue that there were a few exceptions. The brief Stolypin years did at least indicate that there might be a change of attitudes towards the peasantry, and we will never know whether things could have turned out differently. Perhaps this was a missed opportunity, as some historians have maintained, or perhaps Stolypin's reforms were indeed too little and too late.

Again, one might cite the NEP period as a time when peasants were more contented and freer than ever before or since. We will never know what might have happened if Bukharin's solution to the peasant problem had triumphed over Stalin's at the end of the 1920s, just as we will never know whether Khrushchev might have improved the lives of the peasants eventually had his regime not lasted just 8 years. However, all this is to indulge in speculation. The plain fact is that in principle, and very largely in practice, the peasantry remained an exploitable underclass.

Glossary

smychka: Bolshevik propaganda expression of the 1920s to describe the ideological 'link' between the workers (the hammer) and the peasants (the sickle)

Exploitation of the industrial working classes

The word 'exploitation' comes to mind when one considers the treatment of the industrial workers under the tsars and the Soviets, too. However, at least in theory, there was a difference in official attitudes between the tsarist and Soviet regimes. While the peasants were regarded as the 'soul' of 'mother Russia' under the tsars and treated by the Bolsheviks largely as an alien and exploitable class, the industrial workers were treated with suspicion as a hostile class by the tsars and, officially at least, as the 'core' and 'soul' of the great 'socialist future' by the Bolsheviks. The key question here is whether the workers under the Bolsheviks really did benefit as active citizens of the first workers' state in history, or whether they were, at least to an extent, exploited as they had been before 1917.

For most of the nineteenth century, the industrial working classes formed only a tiny minority of the working population. Precise statistics are difficult to obtain, partly because it is difficult to define the working class with clarity. During the later years of the century there was a vast seasonal migration as peasants escaping rural poverty in the dead seasons drifted to towns to find temporary work — so the expression 'peasant-worker' is probably more apt. Moreover, Soviet and other Marxist commentators have tended to exaggerate the size of the industrial proletariat.

It is probably safe to say that by the mid-nineteenth century the factory population was approaching 400,000–500,000. These workers were concentrated mainly in the textile industries around Moscow and the metallurgical industries around St Petersburg. Before 1861 most industrial workers were serfs, operating under draconian rules and in conditions similar to those imposed on their peasant counterparts.

The rate of industrial growth was slow until the 1880s. In 1861 industrial workers formed approximately 0.75% of the population. It was during Witte's 'Great Spurt' that the number of workers rose rapidly. However, by 1900 there were still not many more than 1.5 million workers (1.25% of the population) and even by 1914 there were fewer than 2.5 million (around 1.5%). The percentage of industrial workers remained low because of the rapid rise in the rural population at the time.

The tsarist authorities had difficulty in understanding and classifying industrial workers. The majority of them were still legally classed as 'peasants', the class from which they came. It wasn't until 1884 that senior figures in the Ministry of the Interior, becoming concerned about the potentially dangerous development of a factory proletariat, began to differentiate between the attitudes and mentalities of the workers and the peasants. Even so, by 1900, around 90% of industrial workers were still defined legally as 'peasants' in their internal passports.

A growing awareness of the potential problems caused by this new class was intensified by a series of illegal strikes and walkouts after 1885. This led to differences of opinion between the Ministry of Finance under Witte and the Ministry of the Interior (responsible for policing and the maintenance of public and political order). Witte's policy of rapid industrial growth, with the new factory proletariat being seen as exploitable, much like the peasantry, conflicted with the natural concerns of the Ministry of the Interior. By the 1890s the Interior Ministry was advocating close political surveillance of workers in factories, but the Finance Ministry thought that this would limit potential efficiency and productivity. This conflict betrays a lack of understanding of the conditions of the workers and a lack of any coherent policy in addressing this problem.

The condition of the industrial workers, 1890–1914

While it is true that, particularly during the primary stage of industrialisation, industrial workers in western Europe suffered poor living and working conditions, those in Russia suffered far more. This was partly because of the nature and speed of industrialisation from the 1890s, and partly because of the aforementioned lack of understanding or concern by either the state or private industrialists. Because of the backward starting position, there was a large concentration of industry into large-scale enterprises. By 1895 30% of industrial workers were in factories employing more than 1,000 people. By 1914 more than 40% were in giant enterprises. The huge Putilov armaments and metallurgical factories in St Petersburg were the largest in Europe. This concentration of labour was more than twice that of countries like Britain or the USA. Urban conurbations grew rapidly; the population of Ekaterinoslav grew from 47,000 to 150,000 between 1886 and 1896, and in Rostov-on-Don from 80,000 to 150,000 in the same period. The population in Baku, the oil-producing region, grew from 46,000 to 108,000.

Working conditions

The conditions for this 'half-peasant, half-worker' class are well known. Disorientated through seasonal migration, they were herded together in vast barrack-like dormitory buildings, often sharing beds on a shift basis. With real wages in most industries declining by the 1890s, no access to the few consumer goods produced, high incidences of drunkenness and alcoholism, absurdly long working hours and harsh discipline, the conditions for workers seemed to be deteriorating rather than improving. A vivid, grim portrayal of the condition of the industrial workers is provided by Maxim Gorky in his play *Lower Depths*, written in 1902.

Given that most industry was led and directed by the state and most industrial enterprises were state-owned, one might have expected the state to take some initiative in addressing the problems of the workers. Some state legislation on labour was introduced during the 1880s and 1890s, despite opposition from employers. By 1882 the employment of children under the age of 12 had become illegal. A maximum of 8 working hours per day was imposed for children aged between 12 and 15, and a factory inspectorate was established. In 1884 there were further laws concerning school attendance for child employees, and night work for women and children was forbidden in textile factories. In 1897 a maximum working day of 11.5 hours was imposed for all workers. The practical implementation of these laws depended, of course, on the efficiency and conscientiousness of the factory inspectors, and this was often lacking. However, the state also took the lead in a far more negative fashion. In 1886 penalties for illegal striking were introduced (2–4 months in prison for strikers, 4–8 months for ringleaders). Trade unions had already been made illegal in 1874.

Strikes and recession

It was the growing number of strikes which had led to these government measures. The first important strikes took place in St Petersburg cotton mills in 1878–79. In 1896 there were more serious strikes in the cotton mills, where some 35,000 workers refused to work. By the late 1890s the strike movement was spreading to other industries and other provinces. It is not true to say that the government did nothing to address the condition of the workers, but state legislation was minimal, incomplete and implemented poorly. Government policy remained hostile to workers. The police collaborated with employers in measures for protection of public order in the factories, and the secret police, the *Okhrana*, was employed to spy on potential subversives. The lack of understanding of the workers and the suspicion with which they were viewed by the authorities is illustrated by this comment from the chief of gendarmes in 1901: 'In the last 3–4 years, from the good-natured Russian lad has formed a peculiar type of semi-literate intellectual who considers it his duty to deny religion and the family, to ignore the law, to disobey it and make jokes about it.'

The industrial recession after 1900 naturally made conditions worse. Industrial prices fell, particularly in the metallurgical industries. Unemployment rose and working-class discontent grew. There were increasing numbers of street riots and incidences of violence in industrial cities. This did not lead the authorities to consider any meaningful attempts to improve the conditions of the workers. Indeed, unrest in the factories was met with even more severe repression in the early years of the twentieth century. This increasing urban unrest, and the authorities' response, forms part of the background to the developing revolutionary situation of 1904–05.

It is the famous petition which Father Gapon had intended to present to Nicholas II on Bloody Sunday and the response of the troops which best reveal the extent to which the tsarist authorities treated the working classes as exploitable. It is worth repeating here the first section of the petition, which effectively sums up the situation:

> We working men of St Petersburg, our wives and children, and our parents, helpless and aged men and women, have come to you, our ruler, in quest of justice and protection. We are beggars. We are oppressed and overburdened with our work; we are insulted, we are not regarded as human beings but are treated as slaves who must suffer their bitter lot in silence. We have suffered but are driven further and further into the abyss of poverty, injustice and ignorance; we are strangled by despotism and

tyranny, so that we can breathe no longer. We have no strength at all, O sovereign. Our patience is at an end. We are approaching that terrible moment when death is better than the continuance of intolerable sufferings.

The petition went on to describe the refusal of employers to listen to the complaints of the workers, the poor conditions in the factories, the complete lack of human rights and the total indifference of government ministers and officials to the plight of workers (and peasants). Significantly, the tsar was not blamed for this; indeed, the point of the petition was to bring this plight to his notice. The response of the authorities led to the deaths of hundreds of defenceless men, women and children. This in turn led to further industrial unrest which culminated in the revolution of 1905.

It was during the period 1906–14 that the indifference of the government to the plight of industrial workers became most revealing. In the immediate aftermath of the revolution there was a savage repression with multiple executions of worker-militants in a campaign led by Stolypin. Despite the experiences of 1905, the tsar's government made a few, half-hearted attempts at improving conditions. It did allow sickness benefit funds and accident insurance, but essentially the government's response was what it had always been.

The outcome was a dramatic rise in the number of strikes after 1910. If one assumes that workers in Russia would not go on strike unless they were desperate, particularly since they ran the risk of savage repression, then the statistics are very revealing: in 1910 there were some 232 strikes in the empire, 2,032 in 1912 and more than 3,000 in the first half of 1914 alone. The most notorious of these was in the Lena Goldfields in 1912, where 500 were injured and 170 killed in the savage repression by the troops. Not only was repression of the workers not declining, it was increasing in scale.

The tsarist autocracy clearly treated the industrial workers as an exploitable class in much the same way that it treated the peasantry. At least it can be said that Stolypin made some attempt to tie the peasantry into the regime with the creation of a *kulak* class. There was no equivalent with the industrial workers, and there was certainly nothing like the attempts made by Bismarck in Germany, with his state socialism in the 1880s.

The 'workers' state' and war communism

It is not surprising that the short period of the Provisional Government failed to result in any improvement in working and living conditions. First, the decision to remain in the war meant that the vital questions of interest to industrial workers — wage rises and the 8-hour working day — had to be put off until after the war and elections to a Constituent Assembly. Second, the government, dominated by *Kadets* and *Octobrists*, represented the interests of the industrial, business and middle classes, not those of the proletariat. The workers had to be content instead with some vague promises of 'workers' control' in factories. The government urged them in vain to show restraint in their relations with their employers.

The failure of the Provisional Government to address the demands of the workers and the secondary, subordinate role taken by the Mensheviks helped to pave the way for the Bolshevik seizure of power in October. Clearly, great hopes were invested in the new workers' state, but what was it that the workers wanted? Naturally, they demanded basic things like higher wages and shorter hours. The '8-hour day' had been a rallying call for socialist political parties throughout Europe. However, the Bolsheviks offered (indeed promised) them more than this. With the 'bourgeois state' smashed, workers should take over and run the factories. This would be a state which would be run in the interests of the workers. Thus 'workers' control' became as important as questions of wages and hours. Hand-in-hand with all this was the general assumption that the Bolsheviks would bring the fundamental freedoms and civil liberties long denied the workers by the tsars, and only partially given by the Provisional Government. The early signs were promising; in November 1917 Lenin told the workers: 'Comrades, working people! Remember that you yourselves are now running the state…get on with the job yourselves, from below.' On the day after the Bolshevik coup Lenin said: 'We will now begin to construct the socialist order.' What that 'socialist order' actually meant was considered in Lenin's *State and Revolution*, where he recommended that the new proletarian state should seize the property of the bourgeoisie and hand businesses and industries over to the workers. Any resistance to this would be crushed by the workers' party (the Bolsheviks).

The Second All-Russian Congress of Soviets of October–November 1917 effectively launched the 'dictatorship of the proletariat'. Workers' committees were set up to take over industrial property. 'People's courts' were established. The principle of common ownership of the means of production was established and banks and large-scale industries were nationalised. Elected soldiers' committees took control of sections of the army.

For the average Russian industrial worker, this must have seemed like the offering of paradise on earth. No more mass shootings of striking workers, no more 12–14-hour days working for a pittance, no more oppression by the hated police, or beatings by members of the *Okhrana*. In the conditions of autumn 1917 the prospect of a state run by and for the workers must have seemed a heady one indeed.

However, as the nominal rulers of the new state, the Bolsheviks had to consider more than just the interests of the workers. The famous slogan 'bread, peace and land' meant just that. On the day after the coup Lenin arranged a temporary ceasefire on the eastern front, and this was made permanent by the Treaty of Brest-Litovsk in March 1918. This helped to trigger a bitter civil war in which the Bolsheviks would have to fight for their survival. Attention also had to be paid to the interests of the majority of the population, the peasants, whose interests did not exactly coincide with those of the industrial workers. Moreover, the peace treaty meant a large-scale de-mobilisation, leading to unemployment. By the beginning of the Civil War in 1918, more than half of Petrograd's industrial workforce was unemployed. Industrial unrest and strikes meant that the new government enforced greater discipline in the factories. Importantly, the new workers' factory committees were taken over by the trade unions, and these in turn were increasingly subordinated to government control from the centre. In practice, what all this meant was that the construction of the genuine 'workers' state' had to be subordinated to the realities of the situation and the immediate imperative of political survival.

Not surprisingly, the conditions of the workers continued to deteriorate. There were shortages of food and consumer goods. Even before the onset of the Civil War, workers were increasingly disillusioned and demoralised. Their newly won political freedoms had quickly been eroded. Their new masters were the increasingly numerous members of the newly established political police, the *Cheka*. By 1918 the average worker's real wage was a quarter of that in 1913, and by the middle of the Civil War, it was under 10%. During the Civil War the desperate need for weapons, uniforms and ammunition for the Red Army meant long working hours for low pay, and discipline far harsher than that under the tsars. In February 1921 thousands of workers in Petrograd went on strike. The harsh response to this by strike-breakers from the Red Army, reminiscent of tsarist times, prompted the Kronstadt Rebellion. The demands of the 'Red' sailors of Kronstadt, who had many links among the Petrograd workers, suggested just how far relations between the 'workers' government' and the workers had deteriorated: they demanded freedoms of speech, press, assembly and trade unions, the release of Menshevik and Socialist Revolutionary political prisoners, and an end to the one-party state. It could be argued that the suppression of the rebellion by Trotsky's Red soldiers was as savage as the suppression of Father Gapon's march on Bloody Sunday in 1905.

The situation of the workers under the NEP

During the 1920s the economy revived. Under the 'partial return to capitalism', a free consumer and labour market returned. However, unemployment was high and there were about 1 million workers without jobs in 1926. 'Workers' control' had effectively disappeared with war communism, and conditions for workers in factories continued to be harsh. Wages were still low. Trade unions continued to exist but their powers had been curtailed drastically during the Civil War. Strikes were officially discouraged. Trade unionists found themselves in the absurd situation of attempting to defend the interests of workers in a 'workers' state'. Taking all this into consideration, the basic rights and freedoms of Soviet workers suffered by comparison with, say, those of their counterparts in the boom economy of the USA.

Stalinism and the exploitation of the workers

It can be argued that the exploitation of industrial workers during the Five Year Plans of the 1930s far exceeded anything the workers suffered under tsarist rule. Millions disappeared and suffered unspeakable hardships in the labour camps of the *gulag*, Soviet workers had fewer freedoms than before and they were subject to harsh discipline in the factories. Being late for work, or missing a day's work, or accidentally damaging tools or industrial property could lead to accusations of sabotaging the great socialist enterprise. Workers under Stalin were forced and terrorised into giant efforts on a hitherto unknown scale.

Under Stalin, living standards continued to decline. This was almost inevitable, given the heavy concentration in the first two plans on producer goods industries and the consequent lack of consumer goods. Under Stalin there were effectively no more workers' rights. Strikes were forbidden. Brutal penalties could be imposed for breaking the 'code of labour discipline'. Food prices remained high, there continued be a lack of adequate housing, and food rationing continued into the 1930s. By the end of 1939 basic living standards for workers were lower than they had been under the last effective year of the NEP. None of this should be surprising because, despite this being the world's first workers' state, basic living standards for industrial workers were given the lowest priority in the modernisation process of forced industrialisation in the 1930s.

However, it should be aknowledged that the achievements of the Five Year Plans did not depend on fear and terror alone. There is no doubt that, particularly among the younger workers, male and female, there was a genuine sense of idealism, of constructing the ideal socialist state. This was endorsed heavily by official propaganda, but for many young idealists there seemed to be a genuine willingness to sacrifice material rewards In the construction of the great national enterprise. This was given extra impetus by the fact that as far as the Western capitalist economies were concerned, Marx had proved to be correct. The mass unemployment — some 15 million out of work in the USA, for example — did indeed suggest that there was a 'crisis of capitalism' as had been predicted by Marx. Unemployment was virtually non existent in the Soviet Union during the 1930s.

Some material rewards and incentives had to be provided. The most notable example was the introduction of the *Stakhanovite* movement of 1935. Alexei Stakhanov, the coal miner who had (supposedly) mined 14 times the normal amount of coal in one shift, was used as an example and incentive. Those who emulated him could be rewarded with bonuses, decorations ('Hero of Soviet Labour') and even the possibility of holidays and larger living accommodation.

The provision of material rewards for the individual in a socialist state is, of course, a paradox. Not surprisingly, those who gained individual rewards would be in a minority. Far more in keeping with socialist doctrine was the provision of what might be called 'collective' rewards. Hospitals, schools and public libraries were built. Education was made free and compulsory, and crèches for working mothers were introduced on a scale far exceeding that in the West. By the end of the 1930s, the Soviet Union had more medical doctors per head of the population than Britain. Mainly because of the shortage of labour, opportunities for women in the workforce increased dramatically. By the end of the second Five Year Plan 40% of industrial workers were women, although they had yet to receive wages on equal terms with men.

The Khrushchev era

Khrushchev attempted to provide more food and consumer goods and there is no doubt that basic living standards for industrial workers were better in the 1950s than they had been in the 1930s. A minimum wage was introduced in 1955. However, there continued to be a shortage of housing, wages were still low and there was no significant improvement in basic workers' rights, although under Khrushchev the state resorted far less to the *gulag* and the generally harsh punishments that had forced workers into high production levels in the 1930s. In living standards, though, Soviet Russia continued to lag far behind the West.

Conclusions

Whether one argues that the workers continued to be exploited, were more exploited or were less exploited after 1917 than they had been under the tsars depends largely on one's perspective and on the meaning of 'exploitation'. As has been seen, particularly under war communism and under Stalinism it can be argued that generally the workers were treated even more harshly than under the tsars. Perhaps the best that can be said is that the workers' state after 1917 did bring *some* benefits to the working classes.

Questions
&
Answers

The seven essays in this section are all worked responses to typical questions that may be asked on this module. The answers to questions 4, 5 and 6 are genuine responses by candidates who sat the OCR examination in June 2002. The examiner's comments and marks out of 60 are included. The candidates were all the author's own students.

The best way to use this section is to read each essay and in each case consult both the generic and specific mark schemes. Try to understand why the essay has been placed in the given band (six essays are in band I, one essay is in band III). Look for the key requirements: elements of change and continuity, similarities and differences, cause and effect, reference to the entire 100-year period and relevant and adequate supporting detail.

Question 1

With what justification can it be argued that the only real revolution in the period 1855–1956 was that of Stalin?

■ ■ ■

Mark scheme

The question has a natural focus on Stalin and it is expected that much of the essay will be devoted to the 'Stalin revolution'. However, the question also asks candidates to compare Stalin's revolution with other revolutions or revolutionary movements during the period under question. It is expected that candidates will comment on the ineffectiveness of the developing revolutionary movements up to 1917 and offer some judgement on the impact of the 1905 revolution. Clearly, the impact of the two revolutions of 1917 should be considered. Candidates need not agree with the implications of the question and it is perfectly possible for good essays to argue that the Bolshevik revolution had more impact, although good reasons should be given.

Answers in bands I and II should clearly define 'revolution' in terms of the impact that revolutions had on the lives of ordinary people. Essays in these categories should show how society remained largely unchanged by revolutionary movements before 1917, and how fundamentally changed society was by the 1930s and 1940s. Answers in band III will rely on description rather than offer a sharp comparison and analysis. Essays in bands IV and V will be largely descriptive and offer little by way of comparison between revolutions under the tsars, Lenin's revolution and that of Stalin.

■ ■ ■

Band-I answer to question 1

Modern Russian history has been characterised by revolutionary violence. The development of revolutionary movements in the 1870s following the reforms of Alexander II, the assassination of the tsar in 1881, the development of the 'Russian revolutionary tradition', the revolution of 1905 and the two revolutions of 1917 all illustrate this point. The fall of Nicholas II in February 1917 is seen as the culmination of a sequence of events originating with the emancipation of the serfs in 1861. The Bolshevik revolution of October 1917 is taken by many to be the real turning point in modern Russian history. However, if one interprets 'revolution' to mean a fundamental and drastic change in the lives of millions of the population, then it can be argued that the 'revolution from above' of Stalin in the 1930s was by far the most significant turning point.

The emerging revolutionaries of movements like 'Black Partition' and the 'People's Will' in the 1870s achieved very little. The assassination of Alexander II in 1881 did not bring about the fall of the autocracy but instead strengthened it, and a violent reaction and suppression of subversive activity under Alexander III ensued. In fact, the 'revolutionaries' were confined to a small number of members of the intelligentsia who had very little contact with the broad masses. The revolution of 1905 brought little real change to the powers of the autocracy. Indeed, in the countryside the terror of the 'Black Hundreds' brought its own brand of anti-revolutionary violence. In effect, the word 'revolution' can be applied only loosely to the events of 1905. The main events were confined to St Petersburg and Moscow. The army, on its return from the Far East, was able to crush the remains of workers' resistance and Stolypin completed the reaction and suppression in the following years. The Duma granted by Nicholas II in the heat of revolutionary disturbances in the October Manifesto proved to be a sham. The Fundamental Laws enabled the tsar to retain nearly all aspects of autocratic power.

It is true that the fall of Nicholas II in 1917 meant the end of 300 years of Romanov autocracy, to be followed by a short-lived experiment in Western-style liberal republicanism, but in reality, the lives of millions of Russian peasants and workers remained unchanged. It was the inability or unwillingness of the Provisional Government to address the vital issues of the day — the question of the war, land reform, working conditions, and so on — that mainly led the way to its overthrow by Lenin and Trotsky in October.

Perhaps the expression 'seizure of power' or more simply 'coup' is the more apt description of the Bolshevik revolution. What actually happened was that a small, tightly knit and highly disciplined revolutionary party had seized power in Petrograd in one night, followed by similar occurrences in Moscow a week later. Despite subsequent Bolshevik propaganda portraying the 'storming of the Winter Palace', the population of the capital woke up the morning after the coup to placards around the city proclaiming the arrest of the Provisional Government and the establishment of a Soviet government operating in the name of the workers. The Bolsheviks had captured power in two cities in the vast Russian empire, which was numerically dominated by millions of semi-literate or illiterate peasants who had no interest in the events in the capital, took no part in them and undoubtedly had no knowledge of them. This sequence of events hardly deserves the name 'revolution'. Moreover, 90% of a backward society were unsuited in every way to the kind of Marxist revolution that the Bolsheviks advocated, not even in its adapted 'Marxist-Leninist' form.

Lenin's new government did attempt revolutionary initiatives such as workers' control of industry (soon abandoned) and war communism during the Civil War. However, the introduction of the NEP in 1921, despite it being officially described as 'two steps forwards, one step back', was in reality a concession that the majority of the population — largely the peasantry — was not yet ready for the real socialist revolution.

It was Stalin who achieved this real revolution. During the Stalin era, the Soviet Union made huge progress towards catching up with the West, which had been the object of all regimes since 1855, although it was still lagging some way behind by 1953. It was Stalin who ruthlessly and dramatically changed the lives of tens of millions of peasants who were subjected to collectivisation. Experiments in co-operative farming had begun during the war communism period, but these had been on a small scale and hardly successful. It was Stalin who solved the problem of both the peasants and the *kulaks* once and for all and by 'liquidating the *kulaks* as a class', and achieving a collectivisation of all European Russian farms in the winter of 1930–31, drastically altered the face of Russian agriculture. For the first time the state was able to dictate agricultural production and methods in a way that neither serfdom, the tsarist regimes nor the NEP had been able to do.

Perhaps it was in industry that the most dramatic and fundamental changes came about. The substitution of a planned economy for that of the private market was truly an innovation. The ability of the central government to establish quotas, set targets, impose drastic punishments for failure, and some rewards for over-achievement, helps to explain the extraordinary increase in industrial output in the first two Five Year Plans. The world's first large-scale planned economy was indeed revolutionary. Collectivisation and the Five Year Plans made workers' control and war communism seem insignificant by comparison. It was also during the Stalin period that great progress was made towards educating the population. During the 1930s far more was done in the fields of education and medical technology than had ever been achieved before.

This was all accompanied by ruthless application of terror, and the population suffered many hardships. Millions of workers died or 'disappeared' in the camps. Those who criticised the great 'Stalin revolution', or appeared to do so, were ruthlessly punished. In this negative sense, the Stalin years can also be seen as revolutionary in that the revolution affected everybody in Russia, far more than Lenin's revolution had. By revolutionising industry and agriculture and by mobilising the population by both fear and incentives, it was Stalin, rather than Alexander II, Witte or Lenin, who 'dragged Russia kicking and screaming' into the modern world.

e The essay offers a good definition of what is meant by 'revolution' in this context and examines aspects of revolutions and revolutionary movements throughout the whole period in this light. There is a detailed assessment of Stalin's 'revolution from above', with an explanation of why this can be considered the 'real' revolution. Comparisons are made, naturally, with the Bolshevik coup. Much of the essay is devoted to Stalin and there is nothing on the Khrushchev period, but this is not surprising since the module stops in 1956, too early to assess whether the post-1953 'revolution' had any real importance or impact. The wording of the question implies emphasis on the late tsarist period and comparisons between the Lenin and Stalin revolutions, and this is what is offered here. Within the confines of the question, examples are drawn from across the period. The essay would merit between 55 and 60 marks, making it a high band-I response.

Question 2

'An exploited underclass.' How true is this description of the Russian peasantry during the period 1855–1956?

■ ■ ■

Mark scheme

Candidates should consider developments both before and after 1917. There are plenty of examples of exploitation: the disappointments of emancipation, the use of land captains, the prevalence of famine, the policies of Witte in squeezing the peasantry, exploitation under war communism and, of course, the hardships suffered during collectivisation in the 1930s. Equally, candidates can point to aspects where peasants were not necessarily exploited: technical freedom under emancipation, Stolypin's changed emphasis, some relaxation under the NEP, and Khrushchev's increased emphasis on peasant interests.

Answers in bands I and II will not necessarily consider all these factors but will clearly point to similarities and differences — although far more emphasis is likely to be given to similarities. Good candidates might argue that the peasantry fared slightly better under the tsars but will also point out that there was little difference in principle between the attitudes to the peasantry before and after 1917. Answers in band III will tend to be descriptive rather than analytical and the range of examples will be more limited. Answers in bands IV and V will be almost totally descriptive, with little real attempt to point out common themes and attitudes. Answers which focus almost exclusively on either the pre- or post-1917 period can only reach the top of band V at most.

Band-I answer to question 2

During this whole period, the Russian peasantry was by far the largest social group in Russia and the empire. However, this class has tended to be treated as an 'object' of history. Urban Russians, whether under the tsars or the Soviets, generally adopted a paternalistic and patronising view of the Russian peasant. The word '*muzhik*' implied a good, solid citizen who was not very bright. As a result, whether during the 1860s or the 1950s, the Russian peasantry tended to be exploited and treated as an underclass.

The Russian peasants gained very little, if any, benefit from the emancipation of the serfs in 1861. It is true that they legally gained their freedom after many years of slavery under serfdom, but they were still effectively tied to the village commune, the *mir*. The unexpected redemption payments, the periodic redistribution of the village lands and subjection to the commune for decisions on which crops to grow meant that a large-scale, prosperous and contented *kulak* class would take a very long time to develop. With a rapid rise in the rural population in the second half of the nineteenth century and the high price of land, the majority of Russian peasants faced huge land shortages, poverty and hunger.

The Russian peasantry bore the brunt of Witte's 'Great Spurt' of industrialisation in the 1890s. Witte was far more concerned with industry than agriculture, and has often been accused of neglecting the peasantry. A great deal of the burden of taxation to help pay for imports was placed on an already impoverished peasantry. By the turn of the century, rural Russian poverty and backwardness went hand-in-hand. Stolypin later attempted to address the problem by encouraging the creation of a *kulak* class, and peasants were encouraged to break free of the restrictive commune. A land bank was established to help peasants buy land. However, such was the fundamental conservatism of the peasantry that by 1916 only 20% of peasants had taken advantage of the reforms, leaving the vast majority still trapped in poverty, land shortage and hunger by the eve of the First World War.

During this war and the subsequent Russian Civil War the peasants suffered dreadfully. Essentially, the Russian infantry consisted of peasants in uniform. It was the Russian infantry, poorly clothed, poorly fed, poorly equipped and poorly led who constituted the majority of the millions who were killed or seriously wounded on the eastern front. Having gained nothing from the Provisional Government of 1917, Russian peasants had been encouraged by the Bolsheviks to 'vote with their feet' and take the land for themselves. They were soon disillusioned during the Civil War. The peasantry suffered greatly at both the hands of the Reds (under war communism and the grain requisition squads) and the Whites (who shot peasants for 'collaborating' with the Reds). Whole villages were often razed to the ground by marauding Red or White armies.

It can be said that the peasantry gained some respite during the NEP period of the 1920s. Deliberately aimed to win peasant support for the Bolshevik regime and to enable Russian agriculture to recover, the NEP indirectly encouraged the development of a *kulak* class (although the extent of this was exaggerated by the regime, especially Stalin). However, even during the 'golden years' of the NEP, especially in the late 1920s, the regime progressively squeezed the peasants further by constantly raising the compulsory grain payments to the state.

Undoubtedly the most drastic policy affecting the lives of the peasants was that of collectivisation of agriculture in the early 1930s. Stalin had announced that 'we must liquidate the *kulaks* as a class'. Millions of peasants, whose wealth would hardly qualify them for the description 'prosperous' in the West, were killed or simply 'disappeared' in the camps. Russian peasants, herded forcibly into giant collective farms, were subjected to harsh discipline. The state was now able to dictate and control the requisition of grain from the farms. As a result, the peasants on the whole suffered far more than they had done even in the 1890s. It is true to say that, just as Witte had ignored the sufferings of the peasantry in his industrialisation of the 1890s, so did Stalin in his drastic modernisation of the 1930s. Both treated the peasantry as an exploitable class. In the Ukraine in particular, collectivisation caused dreadful hardships and was detested by the peasantry, as the invading Nazis discovered in 1941.

question

During the nineteenth and particularly the twentieth centuries, Russia suffered arguably more than any other country from the effects of war and famine and it was the Russian peasants who bore the brunt of this. Millions of peasants suffered and died in the famines of 1891, 1920–22 and, most dramatically, 1932. The fact that during the latter famine, Stalin not only failed to stop the grain requisitions which might have alleviated the famine, but actually increased them, speaks volumes not only for Stalin's priorities, but his contempt for the peasantry as an exploitable class. As has been noted, it was the Russian peasantry in uniform which suffered the most in the 1914 war, and in even greater quantities during the Great Patriotic War after 1941. Even under Khrushchev, during the Virgin Lands Campaign, the western Siberian peasants were exploited and coerced into exchanging livestock farming for grain production, causing widespread hardship.

Throughout modern Russian history, therefore, the peasantry has been treated as an exploitable underclass, whether as providers of taxation under Witte, cannon fodder for the tsar's armies, suppliers of grain for the Red Army and urban population under the Bolsheviks, or grain exports under collectivisation. The peasantry paid for the costs of modernisation without reaping any of the benefits.

> 🖉 A wide range of examples drawn from across the period is used to illustrate similarities and differences. There is a consistent focus on exploitation and some balance is provided by the recognition that the peasants were not always ruthlessly exploited. There is regular analysis rather than mere description, and the issue of continuity in basic attitudes towards the peasantry over the whole period is dealt with in the conclusion. Various aspects of exploitation are also considered. The essay would be awarded a high band-I mark of between 55 and 60 marks.

Question 3

'From one autocracy to another.' How far is this an accurate description of the political tradition in Russia between 1855 and 1956?

Mark scheme

The question requires good awareness of the development of the autocratic tradition in modern Russian political history. Candidates will need to demonstrate a knowledge and understanding of tsarist autocracy, how it operated and what this implied in terms of the weakness of liberalism and the tendency for initiatives always to come from above. A good awareness of the reasons why the Provisional Government of 1917 lasted such a short time should be shown, and how, with Lenin's coup and the imposition of Bolshevik rule from above, Russia was in many respects 'reverting to type'. There are many similarities: divine right rule and the cult of personality, use of force and terror, weakness of liberalism, control of the economy from above etc. Differences include questions of scale and ideology.

Answers in bands I and II will not need to consider all the above but will clearly point out the similarities between methods used by the tsars and by the Bolsheviks. Good answers will also point out that the 'autocratic' argument applies rather more to Stalin than to Lenin. Band III answers will tend to describe the traditions of autocratic rule rather than point to similarities and differences. Answers in bands IV and V will be largely descriptive and narrative.

Band-I answer to question 3

Within the space of a few months, from the fall of Nicholas II in February 1917 to the closure of the Constituent Assembly by the Bolsheviks in January 1918, Russia effectively went 'from one autocracy to another'. The experiment in a liberal democratic form of political system was doomed not just because the Provisional Government took the fateful decision to remain in the war, but largely because it was an alien concept in the context of modern Russian history. There was little real opposition to the Bolshevik seizure of power in October, and still less to the ending of any meaningful democracy in January. The imposition of rule from above under Lenin, later perfected by Stalin, was, it can be argued, more of a Russian tradition than Western-style liberal representative democracy. Stalin's methods of rule have often been likened to those of the tsar-autocrats.

'Autocracy', defined as a system of government which places enormous powers in the hands of one ruler who governs from above, had gradually developed in Russia since medieval times. In an empire as vast as that of the tsars' in the nineteenth century, with its huge distances, poor communications, many disparate elements and vulnerability to attack from outside, some form of strong government was needed to keep it all together. The same can be said of the Soviet empire under Lenin and Stalin. Under Nicholas I, autocracy was given force by the doctrine of 'Orthodoxy, Autocracy and Nationality' and underpinned by the Russian Orthodox Church. Under Stalin it was supported by 'Marxism-Leninism-Stalinism' and the building of 'socialism in one country'.

The weakness of the Russian liberal tradition helps to explain the maintenance of autocracy. The Russian middle class was small, socially isolated and lacked any meaningful independence, unlike its Western counterparts. There were no genuine representative institutions until the establishment of the Dumas in 1906. Even then, the Fundamental Laws of Nicholas II demonstrated just how few of his powers the tsar-autocrat had actually given away. Alexander II, a genuine autocrat despite his reputation as the tsar-liberator, had never intended the granting of a national state parliament along with his other reforms during the 1860s. The resulting disappoint-ments and disillusionments among Russian liberals led to the polarisation of Russian politics which characterised the last half-century of tsarist rule. The chance of a genuine 'middle way' evolving in Russian politics was lost and liberalism found itself sandwiched between growing revolutionary violence on the one hand and increas-ingly savage repression, especially under Alexander III, on the other. The consequence was that the Russian people had become used to a paternalistic system of rule from above, which left little scope for decision making from below, an essential compo-nent of liberal democracy. Any form of opposition was therefore illegal and tended to be dealt with ruthlessly. Under the tsars, political prisoners tended to be sentenced to exile in Siberia. Under the Bolsheviks they were dealt with more brutally, but the general principle remained the same.

Hand in hand with autocratic rule went the development of a political police and the use of force and terror. The political police were founded as the Third Section under Nicholas I and by the time of Alexander III had developed into the *Okhrana* with wide powers of arrest and surveillance. The political police under the tsars helped rule Russia by fear and, to some extent, terror. Within 6 weeks of coming to power the Bolsheviks had established their own political police, the *Cheka*, with many former *Okhrana* agents as members. The powers of the *Cheka* were greater than those of its predecessor, but its operational methods were similar. Despite Marxist doctrine, and some of Lenin's own earlier writings, the Bolsheviks, because of the situation they were in during 1918, needed some form of coercive terror organisation, particularly after attempts on Lenin's life, and the opposition they faced during the Civil War. The role of the political police — after 1934 named the NKVD — reached its height under Stalin. During the later 1930s, agents of the NKVD could rule as a vital arm of the totalitarian state; virtually a 'state within the state'. After the excesses of brutality during the 1930s, Khrushchev reduced some of the powers of the political police — now called the KGB — but essentially the tradition of a political police force was maintained.

Another manifestation of autocracy in Russia common to the tsars and the Bolsheviks was the 'cult of personality'. Under the tsars this usually took the form of a kind of mystical worship of the 'tsar of all the Russias' as the 'father of his peoples'. This was particularly true of the peasantry, the great majority of the population, although, after Bloody Sunday in 1905, somewhat less true of the industrial workers. In 1913, the tercentenary of Romanov rule, and on the outbreak of war a year later, tens of thousands of peasants waved icons of the 'little father'. It was the assumption of personal control of the army and the military disasters at the front after 1915 which eroded this faith.

It is true that Marxist doctrine did not advocate autocratic means of rule, and Lenin deliberately avoided fostering a personality cult. This was only developed retrospectively after his death by Stalin. However, Lenin can be said to have possessed an autocratic personality and his means of rule certainly bore many resemblances to autocracy. Policy decisions like the signing of the Treaty of Brest-Litovsk in 1918 and the launching of the NEP in 1921 were forced through from above. At the Tenth Party Congress of 1921, all internal dissent within the party was suppressed in true autocratic manner.

It was under Stalin that autocratic forms of rule most resembled — and surpassed — those of the tsars. With the failure of Lenin's predicted revolutions in other, more advanced states, Soviet Russia found itself alone and vulnerable to invasion in a hostile world This at least was the justification of the absurd cult of personality, the brutal rule by fear and terror, the purging of 'enemies of the state' and the forced rapid industrialisation and collectivisation of agriculture which were the hallmarks of Stalinism. In the circumstances, Russia needed strong leadership from above in a system that simply could not tolerate or afford any form of opposition, criticism or dissent. Stalin was seen as the 'father of his peoples', the 'protector' of socialist Russia, just as the tsars were the protectors of 'Holy Russia.'

There are similarities too in the management of the economy. Witte's 'Great Spurt' of industrialisation in the 1890s was led and directed from above by the state. There was little room for local or individual initiatives. Under Lenin, according to ideology, the state took control of industry and attempted to do the same with agriculture during war communism. During the NEP period there was some relaxation of state control in industry and agriculture, but even then the state retained control of the commanding heights of industry. During the Stalin period the Five Year Plans and collectivisation of agriculture meant a ruthless forcing through of economic development by the state. Although the ideology and sheer scale was obviously different, there are many similarities in the methods and mentalities of the Stalin and Witte periods.

Bearing all this in mind, it is not surprising that effectively Russia went from one form of autocracy to another after 1917. The methods of rule were similar in principle and, of course, there were vast differences between the ideology of the Orthodox Church and Marxism-Leninism, but in many respects the only fundamental difference was the sheer scale and scope of the Lenin and Stalin periods. It is often said that Russia went 'from tsars to commissars'.

question

This essay adopts a thematic rather than a straightforward chronological approach, a tactic which works well. Some of the major themes — police state, terror, personality, weakness of liberalism, management of the economy — are dealt with and in each case similarities and differences between the tsars and Bolsheviks are pointed out. The quality of detail and supporting argument is very good. The question is kept in very sharp focus and the essay shows a high level of synoptic awareness. The essay would gain between 55 and 60 marks, placing it in the higher levels of band I.

Question 4

In the period 1855 to 1956, did the Russian peasantry receive better treatment under tsarist or communist governments?

■ ■ ■

Mark scheme

Candidates should focus on the similarities and differences between the treatment the peasants received, both before and after 1917. Similarities include harsh treatment by both regimes, and being 'squeezed dry' to finance industrialisation. Famine hit in 1891, 1921 and 1932, for example, regardless of regime. Control through the *mir*, land captains and the *kolkhoz* was a common feature, although distinctions may clearly be made. The peasants were given (albeit illusory) glimpses of reform, e.g. emancipation, the Peasant Land Bank and the NEP. Both regimes had a temporary *kulak* policy under Stolypin and the NEP. Peasants were only serfs under the Romanovs until 1861, but candidates may regard this as little more than an exercise in semantics at times. The extent of the peasants' systematic ill-treatment before and after 1917 might be usefully explored.

Candidates in bands I and II are not required to deal with all such issues, but are required to demonstrate sustained judgement. Band-I and II answers will display a high level of awareness of change and continuity, based around a discussion of the similarities and differences between the lives of the peasants under the tsars and the communists. Band III answers will demonstrate satisfactory awareness of change and continuity but will be more limited in the range of evidence used and less well argued. They may contain descriptive or narrative passages. Answers in bands IV and V will be predominantly descriptive or narrative. Alternatively, the analysis offered may be limited in scope.

■ ■ ■

Band-I answer to question 4

It seems that during this period conditions should have drastically changed for the Russian peasantry — the obvious turning point should have been the emancipation of the serfs in 1861. However, the serfs continued to be exploited by both tsarist and communist rule.

The Emancipation Edict in 1861 was brought about because of the crushing defeat in the Crimean War of 1854–56. However, in truth very little changed for the peasants — they became socially freer but no attempts were made to modernise agriculture; rather, the development of a *kulak* class was hindered by the restrictive *mir*, crushing redemption payments, and poor quality and lack of land.

The war with Turkey and the increasing national debt meant that the peasants were again exploited as Alexander III needed to gain revenue, so he heavily taxed consumer goods, forcing the peasants to sell more grain, which resulted in 400,000 dying in a famine in 1891.

The treatment of the peasantry further declined during Witte's 'Great Spurt', 1892–1903, as the peasantry was squeezed for grain exports to fund industrialisation. Thus the peasants were neglected and paid the price for any economic gains — just as they would do under Stalin as he had to fund his Five Year Plans. This led to growing discontent in the countryside, but any revolts, such as the ones in Georgia and the Ukraine, were brutally put down by the government. So, the peasants were denied any voice — and this was also shown through Nicholas II issuing the Fundamental Laws in 1906 following the October Manifesto, and through the closure of the first Duma as it was not to his liking, and the change in the franchise. The peasants were increasingly being exploited and suppressed so that they had no way to object and oppose the regime.

They may have hoped that when the Bolsheviks came to power this would change. After all, there had been Bolsheviks in the countryside during the war encouraging the peasants to 'vote with their feet' and turn against the tsar. Furthermore, they had been promised 'Bread, Peace and Land'. However, just as the emancipation of the serfs in 1861 under Alexander II had provided no real change in the future of the peasantry, so the Bolsheviks continued using many of the tactics employed by the tsars to get what they needed from the peasantry and to force them to conform.

During the Civil War of 1918–21, war communism was used — grain was forcibly seized from the peasants and those who did not conform faced being shot or sent to the new *gulags*. This resulted in a huge famine in which 5 million died. This was even worse than the famine of 1891 after the war with Turkey. So it appeared that Lenin, like the tsars before him, would exploit the peasantry during war (as the tsar had done in the First World War) and would use fear and terror to control them. This is illustrated through Lenin setting up the *Cheka* soon after the revolution, as early as December 1917, and also creating the first labour camps.

These tactics were also used by Stalin. He used terror through the NKVD and labour camps, to force peasant farmers into his new collective farms. He also followed a policy of dekulakisation — millions of peasants who could hardly be considered prosperous in any terms were either shot or disappeared in the labour camps. This seems even more savage and ruthless than any repressive measures used by the tsars. Stalin also resorted to tactics used by Witte during his 'Great Spurt'. He needed huge funds for his Five Year Plans which would industrialise Russia — and the peasantry paid the price for this. Again, the peasantry were squeezed for grain for export, there was a massive famine in 1932 on a scale never seen before, and little was done to help. In fact, Stalin actually increased the grain quotas, which illustrates not only his desperate desire to modernise and catch up with the West, but also that the peasantry were an exploitable class who deserved to be treated in any way the ruler desired. Under Alexander II and Alexander III they were used to fund Witte's 'Great Spurt', during the Civil War they were used to help the Red Army win and those who did not conform were shot, and under Stalin they were used to fund the Five Year Plans and lived in constant terror.

Even when Khrushchev came to power the peasants' wants and needs came second. The workers received improvement in their living conditions and a minimum wage in 1956. However, under the Virgin Lands Campaign many peasants were forced to switch to arable farming, which was not successful and resulted in another famine in 1955.

Through this period the peasantry were treated as cannon fodder. They suffered atrocious losses in the Crimean War and in the First World War, in which 9.5 million had died by 1917. This did not change when the Bolsheviks came to power as they suffered awfully during the Civil War of 1918–21 and millions of Russian peasants died on the eastern front during the so-called Great Patriotic War of 1941–45.

However, some attempts were made to try to help the peasants in this period. It would seem that emancipation in 1861 was a step forward despite the fact that it was largely resented. The peasants' land bank was introduced in 1883, redemption payments were eased and in 1886 the poll tax was abolished under Alexander III. Stolypin's reforms tried to create a *kulak* class but, as so often happened in Russian history, reform was met with repression as any disturbances were brutally put down. It is from this period that the term 'Stolypin's neckties' is derived.

The NEP in 1921 did ease the situation for the peasants, but the grain quotas were periodically increased and this squeezing of the peasantry reached its height under Stalin. The Virgin Lands Campaign may have been an attempt to move forward but it relied on luck with the weather, and unsurprisingly the peasants lacked this.

Thus I suggest that the treatment of the peasants barely changed between tsardom and communism. The peasants remained exploited and any tentative attempts at reform were soon met with reaction. However, under the tsars there was never such savage treatment as under Stalin. Perhaps one could argue that the treatment of Stalin was worse — his predecessors did seem to want to create a *kulak* class even if it was only to cultivate support. However, Stalin brutally liquidated this class. Under Stalin peasants 'disappeared' on a scale never before seen, so perhaps I must conclude that treatment was worse under communist governments.

> *℮* This essay is long and detailed. The candidate has put his/her knowledge to good effect. There is quite a lot of repetition, but on the whole the essay avoids a narrative and descriptive approach. The focus throughout is on exploitation and on the similarities and differences between the ways in which the tsars and the Bolsheviks treated the peasantry. There is regular analysis and synoptic evaluation and there are few irrelevant passages. The examiner placed this essay just into band I and gave it a mark of 49.

Question 5

How far do you agree that a study of Russian government in the period 1855 to 1956 suggests that Russia did little more than exchange Romanov tsars for 'Red tsars' from 1917?

Mark scheme

Candidates should focus on the similarities and differences between the Russian government under the tsars and the communists. Similarities should include autocratic/dictatorial government, the use of terror and centralised control of the economy. Both regimes tended only to reform under pressure. Comparisons could be made between rule by divine right and the cult of the individual. Differences include the fate of the old elite and the Orthodox Church. The regimes were similar but there are differences of scale (e.g. in terms of economic progress and the use of terror). Both regimes aimed to crush opposition, yet the Romanovs were overthrown. Candidates might consider why constitutional democracy did not emerge in 1917. Special consideration could also be given to the period of Lenin's rule and the power struggle that followed, for example by discussing the extent to which Lenin paved the way for Stalin.

Candidates in bands I and II are not required to deal with all such issues, but are required to demonstrate sustained judgement. Band-I and II answers will display a high level of awareness of change and continuity, based around a discussion of the similarities and differences between government under the tsars and the communists. Band III answers will demonstrate satisfactory awareness of change and continuity but will be more limited in the range of evidence used and less well argued. They may contain descriptive or narrative passages. Answers in bands IV and V will be predominantly descriptive or narrative. Alternatively, the analysis offered may be limited in scope.

Band-I answer to question 5

In Russia, until 1917 when there were two revolutions, the Romanov dynasty ruled with three tsars: Alexander II (1855–81), Alexander III (1881–94) and Nicholas II (1894–1917). Under these rulers the system of government was autocratic, which many historians have likened to the system with which the Soviet Union was ruled between 1917 and 1956. There are many themes common to both systems of government and it seems that the 'Red tsars' of the latter period owed a great deal to the previous regime.

The first similarity between these regimes is that they both employed seemingly totalitarian methods. Due to his reforms, Alexander II was forced to become increasingly repressive as a revolutionary tradition began to develop. From 1881 Alexander III's government entered a period characterised as the 'reaction'. Alexander II had been assassinated by a revolutionary group, the 'People's Will', and this caused his successor to undo any liberal reforms, tighten censorship and freedom and establish the *Okhrana*. The tsars in Russian history represent a patriarchal monarch which, as we shall see, has striking similarities with the later leaders of the Soviet Union.

Nicholas II was similarly reactionary and dictatorial. All three tsars had refused to grant a constitution, despite pressure from liberals and other more radical groups. It was only in 1905, under the pressure of a revolution, that Nicholas II granted a Duma to the Russian people. However, this was merely an image which had little substance and there was no real democracy at all. Nicholas II showed his autocratic, repressive nature by events such as Bloody Sunday, when hundreds were killed, and by the way in which he brutally put down strikes (such as the events of 1912 at the Lena goldfield).

So it is through this use of terror and one patriarchal leader who has absolute power that we see a pertinent comparison with the regimes of Lenin and Stalin. It is clear that the methods of these dictators were not constitutional or democratic; indeed, Lenin closed down the Constituent Assembly in 1918 when the votes did not go in the Bolsheviks' favour. We can also see a comparison in the strong-arm methods of both regimes. In December 1917 the *Cheka* was established under Felix Dzerzhinsky and in 1918, as a result of the Civil War, Red terror was used to enforce war communism and put down opposition. Lenin banned factionalism and did not allow other parties, just as there were no other parties allowed until 1905 under the tsars.

However, under Stalin terror and repression were even harsher than under Lenin and the tsarist regimes. Stalin reigned over a complete one-party state and used purges and terror as his method. It seems that these methods were even more effective under Stalin than the tsars as there was little effective opposition. It is in the love shown to Lenin and Stalin after their deaths in 1924 and 1953 that we see a similarity in the respect given to the tsars by the Russian people. Though under Khrushchev there was a thaw, it is clear that his methods (shown by the crushing of the Hungarian Revolt of 1956) showed similarities with those of all the previous rulers.

Another way in which we may draw comparisons between these two contrasting regimes is their treatment of the peasants, industrial workers and national minorities. The way in which Lenin and Stalin used the peasants to get grain for industrialisation, and the treatment of their subjects, makes Lenin and Stalin very similar to their tsarist predecessors. Neither the peasants nor the industrial workers ever had a democratic vote in this period, just as the national minorities were repressed by Alexander II (as in the Polish Revolt of 1863), Alexander III and Nicholas II by reaction and anti-Semitic sentiments, through to Lenin and particularly Stalin, who was fiercely anti-Semitic.

The way in which reform always came from above with Lenin and Stalin may be likened to the tsars of 1855–1917. Stalin's industrial revolution, which took place in the 1930s, compares with Witte's 'Great Spurt' of the 1890s as we see Russia changing because of the rulers, not the subjects. During this period it was the Russian people who served the state rather than the other way round. All of these comparisons show us how the reigns of Lenin, Stalin and Khrushchev may be seen as similar to the Romanov tsars. Though the ideology was different, it may be argued that their methods were the same, which produced the same result.

However, in terms of catching up with the West, Stalin was far more successful and far more repressive than his tsarist predecessors. This, and the lack of opposition that he faced, may show that he was more than a 'Red tsar'.

e This essay is reasonably succinct and deals with a number of similarities. It is generally theme based and demonstrates evaluation and synoptic awareness. The style is slightly flawed in places, but there is a consistent focus on similarities and differences and nearly all the material used is relevant. There is sufficient analysis and focus for the essay to reach lower band I. For a higher mark the analysis would have to be more detailed and sophisticated, with a wider range of examples. It was awarded 50 marks.

Question 6

Trotsky described war as the 'locomotive of history'. How far can it be argued that change in Russia in the period 1855–1956 was caused only by involvement in wars?

■ ■ ■

Mark scheme

Candidates should focus on some of the issues below, all of which could contribute to an understanding of what caused change to happen in Russia in this period and the extent to which war was the 'locomotive of history'. Candidates who do not understand or refer to the phrase 'locomotive of history' will still have available to them the full mark range.

Arguments in support could include how significant reforms followed defeats in war, as in 1905 and 1917 (twice) did revolutions. The impact of the First World War in terms of the overthrow of Nicholas II and then the Provisional Government in 1917 will certainly be discussed. Kronstadt and the abandonment of war communism followed the Civil War. Stalin justified introducing the Five Year Plans because 'old Russia was ceaselessly beaten' and must never be again. However, candidates may argue against this proposition on the grounds that significant changes were introduced when Russia was not at war, e.g. Witte's 'Great Spurt', the Five Year Plans and collectivisation. Defeat in war was rarely the only reason for reforms such as emancipation and the October Manifesto. The revolutions of 1917 were multi-causal and cannot simply be explained as outcomes of defeats in wars.

Candidates in bands I and II are not required to deal with all such issues but are required to demonstrate sustained judgement. Band I and II answers will display a high level of awareness of change and continuity, based around a discussion both in support of and against the proposition that war was the 'locomotive of history' in Russia in this period. Band III answers will demonstrate satisfactory awareness of change and continuity but will be more limited in the range of evidence used and less well argued. They may contain descriptive or narrative passages. Answers in bands IV and V will be predominantly descriptive or narrative. Alternatively, the analysis offered may be limited in scope.

■ ■ ■

Band-I answer to question 6

Russia saw a great deal of conflict throughout the period 1855–1956, both within Russia and outside. Since these wars often resulted in defeat for whichever regime was in power, they usually exposed weaknesses and this precipitated change.

The Crimean War of 1854–56 showed massive weaknesses throughout Russian society, both in military and civilian life. The army reforms under Milyutin during

question

Alexander II's reign were far-reaching in military terms. However, the most significant reforms were perhaps those to do with the peasantry. The emancipation of the serfs caused such social upheaval in 1861 that it was clear that other reforms were necessary. Thus it can be argued that it was the Emancipation Edict rather than the war which actually caused all the reform, although since it was sparked off by weaknesses exposed during the war, the war could be held primarily responsible.

The Russo–Japanese War of 1904–05 was again significant since it was this that perhaps sparked off the 1905 revolution. The autocracy had planned to unite the country by a short, victorious war in the east, but instead defeat brought division and upheaval. The people were already living in dreadful conditions in the cities and dissatisfaction was being spread by revolutionary activists in the factories. However, it was really the Bloody Sunday massacre that sparked off the mass strikes and demonstrations rather than the defeat in the war itself, although the war was significant in bringing the dissatisfaction and anger at the government necessary for a revolution to develop. In addition, if revolution is viewed as a form of civil war, then clearly war did bring fundamental changes. The October Manifesto, which allowed trade unions and established the Duma, was certainly a massive change. Although the Fundamental Laws removed many freedoms, the Duma was a voice for the people and constituted a severe chink in the autocracy's armour.

This weakness was increased massively by the First World War. The tsar's decision to lead the troops himself and leave only the tsarina and the bisexual alcoholic monk Rasputin in charge of the country was disastrous. At a time of war, a country needs a strong hand at the tiller, not an inexperienced and unpopular one. The regime became more and more unpopular as the defeats piled up and, since the tsar was supreme commander of the armed forces, they were all his fault, which further increased opposition. Waves of strikes began, brought about by poor conditions and revolutionary agitation, and the autocracy began to topple. The fall of the autocracy, though, was not entirely due to the war. Although in the short term it certainly was, the preceding generations of harsh treatment by the government cannot be ignored. However, in terms of a 'locomotive' effect, i.e. speeding things up, the war was certainly crucial in bringing about the massive change that toppled the autocracy in the 1917 revolutions.

The Provisional Government also suffered its downfall as a result of its disastrous decision to continue the war. This made it so unpopular that the people turned against it. The Provisional Government was a non-elected body which seemed to be acting against the wishes of the people, i.e. by preventing peasant land seizures. It was a combination of these reasons and the war that brought about the October Revolution and the Bolshevik rise to power. But, again, the Bolsheviks were not asked by the people to take power; they simply seized it, partly for their own ends. Thus it can be said that Bolshevik self-interest was partly the cause of this major change.

The Civil War lasted from 1918 to 1921 and saw a significant change from what had gone before. In manic attempts to remain in power, the Bolsheviks' policy of war communism saw repression on a grand scale, the likes of which had never been seen before. It could be argued that the change to the NEP was precipitated by the war since the dreadful conditions caused by the war communism of the preceding 3 years had to be rectified.

However, it was perhaps the famine of 1921 rather than the Civil War which caused this change. Lenin realised because of the famine that changes needed to be made in agriculture and industry. It is worth noting here too that the Reds won the war. All the preceding wars which had precipitated change had been defeats. The famines under the tsars had also been cause for change since they exposed weaknesses in the system. The 1891 famine perhaps led to Stolypin's reforms in 1906 and also to Witte's reforms under the 'Great Spurt'. However, both of these and almost all the economic policies of the whole period were designed to put Russia on a war footing. Alexander II did not expect a war, but the tradition was to build up the military regardless. His military expenditure was nearly a third of the budget. Witte's 'Great Spurt' was almost totally aimed at increasing military production. Indeed, Witte resented this because it meant greater restrictions on his actions and also valuable resources being wasted on military projects. War communism was designed to gear Russia for war and provide it with the essentials. Stalin's economic policy was entirely designed to put Russia on a war footing.

Stalin said in 1929: 'We are 50–100 years behind the West. Either we make good the difference in 10 years or we will be crushed.' Stalin's Five Year Plans and collectivisation were arguably the biggest change in the whole of Russian history, since they were not simply economic measures but measures designed to create a new breed of people, 'homo sovieticus' — Soviet man. They were possibly the most far-reaching changes ever seen in the world, and were precipitated by one thing: Stalin's paranoia that the non-communist states were plotting against Russia. The purges, the Terror and the economic policies were designed to make Russia ready for conflict. They were to prove effective too since Russia was able to beat off the threat from the Nazis.

The Great Patriotic War, however, precipitated very little change. Stalin was so deeply entrenched in power that he did not need reforms. Russia too was a victor, perhaps suggesting that it is only defeat which brings change.

The de-Stalinisation by Khrushchev was another fundamental change but this was nothing to do with war. Stalin had won the war, but Khrushchev argued that in doing so he had damaged Russia badly. Thus Khrushchev's reforms were more of a reaction against Stalin's policies than against war itself.

So although many of the changes happened after long periods of dissatisfaction or inefficiency, war can often be seen to have sparked them off in the short term. Thus war was the 'locomotive of history', forcing the pace of things along when they seemed to be stagnating, although under Stalin, national conflict was not necessary, merely the threat of it. It is significant too that all the major changes came about as a result of defeats: the Crimean, Russo–Japanese and the First World War were all defeats and precipitated massive social change. The Civil War and Great Patriotic War brought little change since their victories perhaps strengthened the position of the leaders to such an extent that reform was unnecessary to keep them in power. This seems to be another key issue — reforms were mainly instituted whenever a threat

to power came. Alexander III's reaction was a great change precipitated by the terrorist threat, and the October Manifesto was issued in response to the threat from the workers after the 1905 revolution. Since the communist power was never threatened as a result of the purges, there was no need for reform.

> ✍ This essay contains some excellent discussion and high-level analysis, and uses a wide range of material and examples. The focus throughout is on the question of war precipitating change. There are no irrelevant passages and no merely descriptive or narrative passages. The essay adopts a broadly thematic rather than purely chronological approach, and this helps with the depth and quality of analysis. The approach in the essay satisfies the requirements of the module. This is a good example of a high-grade 'synoptic' essay. It was given a mark of 57, placing it in band I.

■ ■ ■

Band-III answer to question 6

It can be argued that change in Russia in this period was caused primarily by involvement in wars. War provides change as it outlines the flaws in the system. However, there are other factors that determine change, including an increase in free thinking (due to education and Western influence), the need to compete on an international basis economically, and to improve the standards of living of the population.

The Crimean War that ended in 1956 [*sic*] showed the flaws in the Russian system. The tsars had run on the complacency obtained from victory against Napoleon 60 years beforehand. This was a great shock. The war thus contributed towards the decision for emancipation in 1861 and the other reforms. This included the reform of the army under Milyutin and the social reforms in the judicial, prison and education sectors such as the university statute of 1863. It can be argued that these reforms increased expectations both domestically and in the nationalities of Finland and Poland, leading to an increase in free thinking and revolutionary activity, i.e. the Polish Revolt of 1863 and the rise in influence of revolutionary organisations such as 'Land and Liberty' and the 'People's Will' (which were ultimately responsible for the assassination of Alexander II in 1881). These factors can all lead back to war. The Turkish war of 1877 showed to an extent how the reforms had worked, although Moltke said of the war: 'It is like the one-eyed (Russia) beating the blind (Turkey).'

The Russo–Japanese War of 1905 was an attempt to obtain a measure of glory abroad, thus uniting the people in a patriotic well-being. However, this once again showed up the inadequacies of the Russian system. This war contributed to the revolution of 1905 and the reforms that followed — for instance, the creation of the Duma, which was a landmark in Russian history despite its weaknesses.

The First World War of 1914–18 perhaps provoked more change than any other in history. Russian losses and poor leadership from Nicholas II contributed to the lack of food and distrust in the system. This led to the abolition of 300 years of Romanov rule and a 'democratic' Provisional Government. This is undeniably a massive change.

The Civil War occurring between 1918 and 1921 consolidated and cemented the position of a communist government in the largest state in the world. It also had the effect of undermining the peasantry through war communism. This led to Lenin's NEP which was once again a large change as it introduced capitalism. It also helped cause the famine of 1921, caused indirectly by the Civil War.

War can, however, also be seen as a measure of strength. The Second World War showed Stalin's collectivisation to have worked. Although the war went badly up to the battle of Stalingrad, it showed that Russia was once again a major power. A lot of the economic strides made in the 1930s and 1940s were in preparation for war with the capitalist West and so change was provided this way. However, due to the intense paranoia of Stalin, war also changed the nature of the Communist Party. He purged millions of people due in part to his fear of international attack and war. One outcome of the Great Patriotic War was the emergence of the very strong powers (superpowers), the USA and the USSR. This was to lead to a conflict of interest between communism and capitalism and eventually to another form of war — the Cold War.

This particular 'war' provoked huge changes. Russia really did have to compete with the West now on many different levels. On a military level, the nuclear arms race developed, leading to mutually armed destruction [sic] (MAD). On a level of prestige it encouraged the space race, as communism had to be shown to be efficient, and on a social level it resulted in Khrushchev's attempt to produce consumer goods through his Seven Year Plans. However, these measures took a massive toll on Russia's economy. The peasants were forced to pay and simply could not afford it. Khrushchev said in 1956 that in 3 years he wanted to produce more grain than any other country. Within 2 years he was importing grain from the USA. Russia simply was not in a position to compete with the USA. It is thus clear that the Cold War provoked serious change.

Although it is apparent that to an extent war is the 'locomotive of history', this statement is by no means all-embracing. Russia was also changed by a change in the structure and thinking of the population — through increased levels of education, e.g. Golovnin under Alexander II, the university statute of 1863 giving autonomy to universities, the size of the middle class and *raznochintsy* increased, producing revolutionary thought. This obviously caused much change both in terms of the various revolutions or assassinations and in the form of reaction by the tsars and repression by the communists.

Finally, change may have occurred in any case due to genuine humanitarian reasons. Many of the tsars felt truly paternalistic towards their subjects and wanted to improve conditions. Alternatively, change could have occurred for the sake of industrialisation. Every country wants/needs to develop in order to survive. This may not be with reference to war but perhaps economic survival on an international basis. Russia had a huge comparative advantage in raw materials and cheap labour and change was needed in order to exploit this.

In conclusion, it is apparent that war did contribute to a lot of the change in Russian history. It provoked industrialisation due to a fear of inferiority to the West. This was true of both systems, tsarist and communist. War was the international measure of strength. It was used as a domestic policy tool, with the Russo–Japanese War of 1905 being used to quash revolutionary activity (although this rarely worked). However, its repercussions were severe, with the famine of 1921 being a result of the Civil War. Trotsky was correct in his statement. Change was clearly going to be spurred on by war in a country that was powerful, proud, yet at the same time so weak.

𝑒 This essay is not always clearly focused, although it does show some synoptic development. Genuine links between war and change are made, but some of the assertions are rather tenuous. There are several factually dubious statements and the essay rather loses its way in the section dealing with the Cold War. Post-1956 developments are outside the requirements of the specification for this module and the demands of the question and are therefore irrelevant. The English is weak in places. There needs to be a much sharper focus on the question of change and continuity to go higher than band III. This essay was given a mark of 38.